AF482066

Published in the USA by:
BearManor Media
4700 Millenia Blvd.
Suite 175 PMB 90497
Orlando, Florida 32839
www.bearmanormedia.com

Hardcover: ISBN 979-8-88771-057-0
Paperback: ISBN 979-8-88771-056-3

Printed in the United States of America.
Book design by Brian Pearce | Red Jacket Press.

THE LIFE AND CAREER OF Cleo Moore

RICHARD KOPER

AUTHOR OF FIFTIES BLONDES:
SEXBOMBS, SIRENS, BAD GIRLS AND TEEN QUEENS

TABLE OF CONTENTS

This book is dedicated to Debra Lee

ACKNOWLEDGMENTS

I would like to thank Cleo's daughter, Debra Lee Heftler and Cleo's favorite nephew, who wants to stay anonymous. Furthermore, my gratitude goes out to: Connie Ray Hodgeson, Luther Jerry Diez, Kerry Diez Larson, Melissa Hood Duhe, Wendy Ortego, Lisa Causey Babin, R.E. Babin, Marie McCarthy, Jan Lowell, Mamie Van Doren, Terry Moore, Gloria Pall, Kathleen Hughes, Karen Sharpe, Melinda Markey, Kathy Marlowe, Laurie Mitchell, Travis Kleefeld, Christopher Riordan and Steve Hayes for all their help, information and for taking the time to talk with me. Many thanks to Brian Pearce for his creativity and ability to make this, and three of my other books, look fabulous.

Also, a word of gratitude to: Kyle Preston, who granted me to use several photos from his collection, and Veronika Zýková, who provided me with a (Czech) copy of Cleo's long-lost movie *Thy Neighbor's Wife* and Milan Hain, the author of a monography about Hugo Haas and his films.

ARRIVING AT THE RAILROAD STATION
IN ROCHESTER, NEW YORK, PROMOTING
WOMEN'S PRISON, 1955.

PREFACE

While researching I learned about the secret Cleo Moore and her family had kept, and I realize it is a delicate topic to be revealed. In my professional life I am working with families experiencing trauma and communication problems. From a systemic view I see why some people in the first circle around Cleo want to keep the secret theirs. The revelations in this book are not made to shame or blame. I am not in that position and more strongly I don't believe that's how we must look at family secrets and the people that keep them. You cannot force people to talk about the bruises and dark pages in their family history, especially when the hurt is still there. I understand that a book about their famous and beloved family member is welcomed, but making statements and quotes is too vulnerable and confronting.

In my research I tried to get as close as I could to Cleo Moore. Her surviving sister, Jonnie Mae, was still around when I did research for this book. Jonnie Mae did not respond to my letter or telephone calls. Cleo's daughter Debra Lee reacted to my messages on Facebook, but suddenly I lost contact with her. A few years later, late 2020, through a childhood friend, I came in contact with Debra Lee again. I must say this time she was sweet and interested and she offered to talk to me. The interview never happened. Assumably, Debra thinks it is better to be silent about her past and her mother's life. Through one of Cleo's nephews, I came closer to get in contact with Jonnie Mae, but to no avail either. He told me, and I respect what he is saying, that his is a very private family. He is quoted as Cleo's favorite nephew because he wants to stay anonymous.

Cleo had a large family. In the second and third family circle I found some wonderful people who were more than willing to help me getting to know their respected friend and relative. Through them I learned how special Cleo Moore was. The people I talked to, who met her and who worked with her, all share this view. Cleo's intelligence, professionalism, respect for her loved ones and environment are the highlights of the remembrances of Cleo Moore.

I enjoyed my journey getting to know the lady from those wonderfully entertaining Hugo Haas movies. While discovering the woman behind the actress, luring from the film posters and smiling from magazine covers, I became even more intrigued by the person behind the 'bad blonde' guise.

While reading this book, I hope you will get to know the private Cleo Moore better, understand her choices and forgive her 'mistakes.' She deserves to be remembered with a good thought.

Sources are mentioned within the footnotes, when not credited the source was a sole article clipping with no reference to the original publication.

INTRODUCTION

"THE ETERNAL RUNNER-UP"

"THEY ARE HARD ON BLONDES. THEY SEEM TO ASSUME, FOR SOME REASON, THAT BLONDES CAN'T ACT."
PICTUREGOER MAGAZINE, NOVEMBER 1954

Cleo Moore had to fight for everything in her life. She reached fame and recognition through hard work and determination. From a young age she focussed on how to better her living circumstances. She wanted to be in the spotlights, to be someone. Cleo Moore, Louisiana's own Blonde B-movie Bombshell, was born in poverty, but raised in a loving and caring family. A strong community sensed environment nurtured the young girl and helped her to grow into a strong-willed, sensitive woman.

Cleo mentioned about her determination to become famous: "My conditioning for this all-consuming business started very early. In Louisiana, I studied everything that I felt would help me as an actress. I was in every play in which I could get a role, I read volumes on drama and acting, and I took photography, airbrushing and painting so I'd know all about angles, colors, light values and so on. I was the queen of the athletic festivals and other annual events, but I didn't have time for any social activities, because I was always working on something connected with the theatrical world."[1]

Cleo's first-cousin, ninety-year-old Luther Jerry Diez, remembers her fondly. "From my perspective she was a very nice person. I don't know anything bad about her. She was a good person, friendly, always ready to help.

1. *Hollywood Stars,* 1955.

She was kind of obsessed with how to get a better life. She was having her own line of under-clothes. I understand she did very well. She had married someone that was in construction, and I understand he was pretty well-off. She got started in business and I was told she was doing very well."[2]

In the mid-1940s Cleo came to Hollywood and in 1949 she was picked up for a starlet contract at RKO. Mamie Van Doren, at the time an eighteen-year-old RKO starlet, remembers, "I never knew her, but admired her from afar. She was a tad before my time. I used to see Cleo at the boxing matches every Friday night at the Hollywood Legion where my dad had seats."[3] An RKO talent agent had noticed Cleo at the boxing games. RKO signed her and featured her in supporting roles, in dramas and westerns. For a short time, in the early fifties, Marilyn Monroe and Cleo were the hottest blonde starlets in town. They were both tested for a contract at 20th Century-Fox and auditioned for the same parts. When Cleo was hired by director Hugo Haas to star in his

DINKIE GRIPS COLLECTORS CARD, 1945.

independently-made movies, Marilyn signed a contract at Fox and received a big build-up as Fox's number one blonde bombshell.

Cleo was over the moon when Hugo Haas considered her to replace Beverly Michaels, as his leading lady. This was her big step forward, leaving the ingénue roles in B-movies behind her. In 1969 she commented in a rare interview, "I made a number of pictures, strictly C-pictures that were done on small budgets with a crackerjack director and actor who's now dead, Hugo Haas. Anything I learned about the fine art of acting I learned from Hugo. We made one film called *Thy Neighbor's Wife*, in which

2. Source: telephone conversation with author.

3. Source: email contact with author.

I got flogged at the public whipping post for adultery. I did my best acting in that film, I guess."

Actress and screenwriter Jan Lowell, then known as Jan Englund, worked with Cleo on several Hugo Haas movies. She remembered that "Cleo was passable as an actress, just that. She was a sweet, friendly person

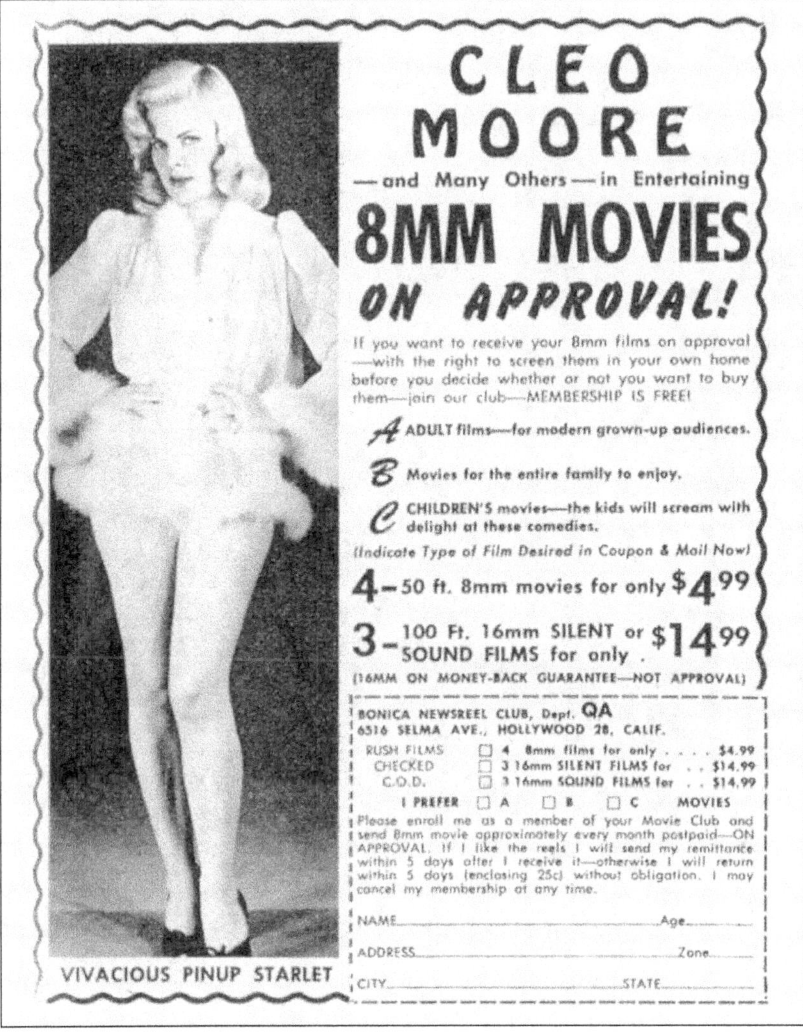

who would do anything to help you. I liked her very much. She enjoyed eating, laughing, having fun. She would not kill a fly. I once saw her catch a bee in her hand and carry it outside to free it. Hugo always gave me a bit in a film when he could. Never a big role because I was not his sort of actress. I was more of what my agent called, an Ida Lupino type. Heavy drama. I had fun and enjoyed being on the set, especially because my husband was there in production. As for Cleo, she was a great gal. Warm hearted, open, and friendly. We were friends on the set and off it as well and we were even invited to her home to meet her family. I liked her."[4]

SIGNED PHOTO FOR CHILDHOOD FRIEND MARGIE DIEZ AND HER HUSBAND, 1951.

Melissa Hood Duhe and her parents visited the Moore's in California. Melissa's mother had encouraged Cleo to go to Hollywood. They were very proud of the star-status Cleo achieved. Melissa remembers that Cleo took her and Jonnie Mae, who was about the same age, to the movie studios in

4. Source: email contact with author.

the early fifties. There she met Groucho Marx, who was filming *A Girl in Every Port* with Marie Wilson at RKO studios. "Cleo took me, my father and mother to her studio and introduced us to Groucho Marx. Groucho had a daughter named Melissa and he joked with us having a daughter with the same name. They took us on a tour through the studio and I got to see how films were made. I was googly-eyed at all the surroundings." Melissa remembers that Cleo's youngest sister Jonnie Mae was a little bit taken aback by Cleo's fame and her famous friends.

MISS BILLBOARD OF 1955.

Cleo knew the value of publicity. Now her name was made she had to make sure that she would dominate the headlines if she wanted to prolong her career. She was named the honorary city siren of Tarzana, California in 1954 and crowned 'Miss Billboard' in Las Vegas, Nevada in 1955. Admittedly, these were the various worthless beauty titles starlets received to obtain publicity. "Keeping yourself attractive isn't just for actresses. No matter what kind of job you have, or even if you are a housewife, you owe it to someone, as well as to yourself, to keep up a good appearance. Looks and personality are so closely tied together that it can't help but make you more interesting and charming, knowing that you are attractive and look your very best." In interviews Cleo wanted to portray herself as the 'wholesome girl next door." The public image she created as the approachable, yet intelligent country girl, contrasted with the bad girl roles she played. When Columbia signed her, she was afraid they were going to change her image. "I was afraid the studio would decide I needed to be changed — make me cut my hair. I especially wanted to keep it long. With everyone wearing short hair, I thought this would give me a certain amount of individuality.

Fortunately, all they did was lighten my hair."[5]

When Cleo's fame grew, she kept paying respect to her roots and simple background. She visited her friends and relatives in the South on a regular basis. Melissa Hood Duhe mentions that "Cleo was very family-oriented. When she would come here, in Galvez, she would always bring studio pictures of herself and sign them and give them out. My father was drawn to Cleo's beauty and he would kiss her, which made my mom so angry. She

5. *The Philadelphia Inquirer*, March 4, 1955.

Hollywood, California
May 12, 1953

Ann Smith,
321 Richard Street,
Dayton 10, Ohio

Dear Ann:

     I received your very nice and sweet letter.
Thank you so much for it. I am so glad you saw
my movie and liked it. I have another one which
will be playing very soon called, "Thy Neighbors
Wife". I hope you will see it too.

     Ann, I am sending you a ballot on which you
will see I am running for Mayor of Tarzana. If
you will please vote for me and return it to the
Tarzana Chamber of Commerce.

     I am having some new large pictures made so
if you would like to have one of them will you
please write again. Thank you so much!

                              Sincerely,

                              Cleo Moore

would have to pretend that everything was fine. She loved Cleo so much."[6]
Melissa remembers that Cleo was somewhat uneasy with her newfound
fame and all the attention that she gathered. She describes Cleo as humble,
very friendly and stresses that she had no star allures what-so-ever. Her
favorite nephew recalls that, "She was loquacious, fun loving, extroverted,

6. Source: email contact with author.

family oriented, and very loving! She doted on me. Once she married and moved to Beverly Hills I did not see her very much. I would say she lived a fairly quiet life in the late 1960s and 1970s."[7]

Apart from her family and friends, Cleo also showed her admiration for those who were working in the movie industry behind the scenes. She once commented, "I think perhaps the greatest rule of all is to take your work seriously but never yourself. There are wonderfully competent people in every department — writing, direction, make-up, hairdressing, etcetera — to do that kind of worrying for you. I believe in letting them do their jobs and sticking to my own, which is just to give the best performance I possibly can in every assignment."

In the mid-fifties, Cleo saw the rise of other blonde actresses and found new competition in Kim Novak, Mamie Van Doren, Anita Ekberg and Jayne Mansfield. In 1956 British blonde Diana Dors also made her entrée in Hollywood. A British film fan wrote a letter to *Picturegoer* magazine. "Why does Hollywood fuss over Diana Dors when it already has Cleo Moore? In *Over-Exposed* she proves she is better looking, has a better figure and acts Dors off the screen."[8] Without doing injustice to Diana Dors or others, the writer was right in part. Why was Cleo always overlooked by producers and surpassed by new faces, some with less acting experience? *Bold* magazine placed an article in their March 1957 issue. They rooted for the talent Cleo possessed. "Someday, they'll "discover" Cleo Moore. Someday, they'll speak of this "exciting new screen personality" and of her "overnight success." Success is always supposed to come overnight. The truth is rarely admitted — that for most stars, as for Cleo, fame is a hard-fought, elusive goal, and many girls drop forgotten by the wayside. As for Cleo, her career so far has been playing Bad Girls in a succession of B films. Critics, even though they disliked everything else in the "potboilers," admitted she showed acting ability. But nothing happened. No Prince Charming came offering a top-notch role. Instead, the B roles went on and on. Now, Cleo has saved enough to finance her own movie, and will find out if this gal Moore really has what it takes to become a star. Odds are she'll make it. Perhaps unknowns just step casually into leading roles. Perhaps. But more likely, most stars have backgrounds similar to Cleo's — for only from such hardships are real actresses born."

Cleo never reached the height of stardom she had hoped for and by 1956 her film career was over. She stayed on in Hollywood for a while,

7. Source: email contact with author.

8. *Picturegoer*, December 29, 1956.

trying to re-activate her career. A visit to Florida for pleasure- and business purposes, proved to be a life changing endeavour. From an early age, and throughout her time in Hollywood, Cleo pronounced that she would run for governor of Louisiana in the year 1960. Considered a publicity hound, her actions and publicity stunts sometimes garnered a negative reception. The still remembered five-minute kiss proved to be her most (in)famous outing of gaining attention. "Cleo, by the way, is the girl who got disc jockey Jack Eigen fired for holding the longest kiss in the history of

CLEO AND MARGIE DIEZ (RIGHT).

television. She really pressed those lips and kept a firm clutch. Cleo is also the girl who threatens to run for the Governorship of Louisiana, her native state. She promises this whenever her headline ratings drop to a new low."[9]

Her final years were spent in Beverly Hills. Living with her daughter Debra. Debra's high school friend Marie McCarthy mentions, "I loved Cleo and it would be nice for someone to write about her. Hopefully not

SIGNING AUTOGRAPHS IN 1954 (LEFT) AND AUGUST, 1955 (RIGHT).

focusing on the darker side because she truly was a beautiful, sensitive, and talented soul who loved her daughter very much. She used to tell us as kids that we could live with her forever."[10]

But forever was not meant to be. Cleo died in her sleep, just a week away from her fiftieth birthday. She left a legacy, still loved by aficionados of 1950s Bad Girl Cinema. She would not have foreseen her enduring popularity and the ever-growing interest in the movies she appeared in.

Thirty years after Cleo's passing, her native state Louisiana paid her tribute when a musical cabaret by The Southern Jeze-belles, featured Cleo Moore as one of the "Loose Ladies in Louisiana History."[11] It is about time Cleo's story is told. She was a remarkable lady; she worked hard to be a good daughter, spouse, mother, actress and businesswoman. And in many ways, she succeeded.

9. *The Lowdown*, March-April 1956.

10. Source: email contact with author.

11. Played at *The Shim Sham Club* in February 2003.

CLEO CIRCA 1942.

DREAMS

On Halloween, October 31, 1923, Cleo Una Moore was born in a one-room cabin, on Port Vincent Road, in Henderson Bayou in Galvez, Louisiana. Galvez is an unincorporated community in Ascension Parish, ten miles southeast of Baton Rouge. Cleo's mother Una Causey was fifteen years old when she gave life to her first-born. Cleo's father, Murphy Charles Moore, was twenty-two. Both her parents were descendants of Irish settlers who immigrated to the United States in the 1800's. Murphy was a farmhand and worked together with his brother-in-law Donald Causey. Donald was Una's one-year-older brother. He was married to Ora Causey. Ora and Donald were first cousins. Cleo grew up with their daughter Alice, who was one year younger.

The families lived in a house with no indoor toilet, no electricity, and no gas or running water. Summer or winter, water was pumped from a cistern. Kerosene lamps provided light and wood stoves provided heat. They called it a box car house. It was made from one-inch boards, and it had a tar paper roof which wasn't very high above your head. Over these cracks, where two boards came together, they put a slat to keep the wind from coming through. It was cold in the winter and hot in the summer. It was the poorest excuse for a house, but everyone lived like this, so people didn't pay much attention to it. Some neighbors lived in two-room cabins, with a kitchen.

Alice Causey's son Luther Jerry Diez recalls, "Cleo's mother, Una, and my grandmother were first-cousins. They always stayed together. My mother and Cleo were about the same age, they were very close. I knew her whole family. Cleo had a house, and right behind her house, her backyard and my grandmother's backyard were together. We were all poor. The whole house, we kept it plain. I was born in a little old shag. That's what we lived in."[1] The Moore's lived a typical rural Southern life. Almost everyone in their community was poor. The people milked their cows, raised chickens, planted fields of corn, potatoes, beans and other crops and once a year when the weather was cool, butchered the hogs. Although life as a tenant farmer was hard, nobody ever starved in Galvez.

Within these harsh but simple circumstances, Cleo grew up to be a lively, generous, and well-behaved girl. Because of her sunny nature, people liked being around her. As a family the Moore's were very close. They were warm and generous people. Every Sunday the whole family attended the worship services at the First Baptist Church in Gonzales. Cleo also attended, and when she got older, taught Sunday School. Connie Ray Hodgeson (1930) saw Cleo and her family at church every Sunday. He was the younger brother of Cleo's neighbourhood friend Margie Fay Hodgeson. "Cleo was a very good friend of my sister, who was nine years older than me. They graduated together. Cleo was a country girl. She was very pretty. The Moore's were very poor, they didn't have anything."[2]

In general Louisiana was a very poor state but the degree of poverty in Galvez was extreme. The 1930 census shows that one-fifth of White Louisianans were illiterate, with rates for Black Louisianans being much higher. The Moore's and their relatives were deeply involved in Democratic politics. They also believed in education and, unlike other families in the South, made sure that their daughters would attend school. Politics, in Louisiana, was an all-consuming passion with a lot of families in the 1920s and 1930s. As someone who was born and grew up in Galvez, Murphy Moore inherited all of the resentments of its people against the elite in Baton Rouge who ruled Louisiana. It was the state senator Huey Long, a Democrat and socialist, who wanted to do something about the poverty and illiterateness in Louisiana. The Moore's strongly supported him.

After a working day, the families gathered and talked politics and how the average farmhand was left to starve by the government. In the late hours, when Cleo was lying awake, she would listen in when her relatives started to whisper and talk about Una's infamous cousin Charles Floyd. Charles was four years older than Cleo's mother. He had robbed a Saint Louis grocery payroll when he was twenty years old. He was caught and spent three-and-a-half years in a Missouri penitentiary. After his release he continued his violent robberies. Floyd was a wanted man in states

1. Source: telephone conversation with author.

2. Source: telephone conversation with author.

across America's farm belt. He became a legend with the farmers, tearing up mortgages and giving money to the poor.[3]

In Depression America, Charles 'Pretty Boy' Floyd was considered a kind of hero, celebrated in movies and song. As a young girl, Cleo idealized her mother's cousin too, thinking of him as a kind of Robin Hood. When she asked Una about him, she was told not to speak of him or his relation to her mother in public. At a young age, Cleo learned the importance of keeping a secret. Feeling Una's shame made it even more urgent to keep her promise to never talk about him with others.

When Cleo was seven years old, her sister Yvonne Inez was born. Connie Ray Hodgeson remembered, "Cleo had a younger sister, about my age. I liked her pretty good. I went to the movies with her, a cowboy show. We sat together; we didn't do anything. We were so young, about seven years old." Una Moore raised her two daughters with a firm hand. Cleo and her sister were given a strict religious upbringing. It was an old Southern custom to teach a girl how to cook and sow at a very young age, teaching her the household chores and preparing her for marriage around the age of fifteen. Una made all the girls' clothes herself, but when the Great Depression hit the USA in 1929, Sheriff Lester Gonzales of Ascension parish recalled he had seen Cleo with an all-day sucker in her mouth and wearing a torn dress.

Like many children, Cleo escaped to the movies. At school she loved to take part in various stage plays. She had her first part when she was four. It was a pantomime in which she played a forget-me-not. At an early age Cleo became more interested in how movies were made and how the images of her matinee idols were cultivated and sold to the public. "When I was eight years old, I would go to the movies and just sit and study angles and photography. The other kids were interested in the plot. Then I began taking part in school plays. At first I was the Butterfly or some flower or other."[4]

Cleo adored Jean Harlow. She made a promise to herself that she would work hard to become wealthy and live the life of a movie star. "Ever since I was a little girl growing up on the outskirts of Baton Rouge, I have daydreamed about becoming a movie star." She kept it a secret, afraid the other kids would ridicule her dreams. Cleo participated in grammar school plays, all the time preparing herself for a future career by taking lessons in professional dancing. She dreamed of the life she could have when she

3. 'Pretty Boy' Floyd was eventually cornered by the FBI and shot to death in 1934.

4. *Times-Picayune*, August 12, 1948.

grew up; waiting for it to happen felt like an eternity to her and she longed to escape from her simple rural existence.

In 1936, Cleo was twelve years old, another sister was born. Her parents called her Mary Lea. While five-year-old Yvonne played with the new baby, and Una adjusted to the new situation recuperating from childbirth, Cleo attended Gonzales High School. Gonzales High was a three-story brick building. It housed grades one through eleven. Cleo spent her elementary school years and her freshman and sophomore years of high school there. She was a grade-A student, a bright girl with interest in many subjects. Learning new things and studying for her exams made her happy. Being with her friends and peers fulfilled her with pleasure.

The students brought lunch to school either in a bag or a syrup pail, and weather permitting, Cleo and her friends sat on the grass under a shade tree for lunch. The only thing to drink was water that flowed from a pipe with holes that ran parallel to the ground. Several kids could drink at once, but if some wise guy stopped up a hole, the water shot up higher to the surprise of the next person. As at home, the toilets were outside. Together with the other girls Cleo played Ring Around the Rosie, Hopscotch and Dodge Ball. Because of the segregation, the Gonzales School for Colored was located on Airline Highway, far away from the white school. There was no interaction between the two groups of teenagers. Melissa Hood Duhe, the daughter of Una's friend Regina Hood, grew up in Galvez too. "We were very poor. Our primary income had to do with strawberry farming. In fact, the schools had their school year based on when the strawberries would get picked. In other words, instead of it being like nine months of school and then three months of summer, the time off from school was during strawberry season, around March, April."[5]

The Strawberry Festival was a big event. Riding the Ferris Wheel was a great joy to Cleo and the other kids. Strawberries were plentiful and prizes were awarded to farmers who competed. Many citizens donated chickens, eggs, and potatoes to the local fairs, reducing expenses. In Summer everyone stayed out all evening. It was cooler outside because no one had air conditioning. In the fall Cleo and her friends would go to the tent skating rinks that would come to Gonzalez. After school Cleo helped her parents in and around the house with different chores. In their spare time, Cleo, Alice and Margie, went to the Pasqua Theatre to see a movie or visited Dar's Café to eat their famous hamburger and to listen and dance to their jukebox. After an early show, Cleo and her friends went on to a night

5. Source: telephone conversation with author, 03-17-2020.

of dancing. Saturday nights at Cedar Grove Nightclub featured popular bands such as Claiborne Williams, the Creole Serenaders and The Black Devils. The girls jitterbugged to Benny Goodman's *Don't Be That Way* and slow danced to Glenn Miller's *Moonlight Serenade.*

Cleo's physical development had started at the age of ten. Fully developed thirteen-year-old Cleo started getting the attention of the older boys around town. "I matured at an early age and it made me very self-conscious to be wearing a bra in classroom full of lanky, flat-chested schoolgirls. It left me with a shyness that was hard to overcome."[6] Eventually, Cleo got more self-assured and flaunted with what nature had given her. With her big eyes, dark brown curls and broad smile, Cleo was quite a looker. Her hourglass figure made her popular with the boys. At different times she had been 'Queen' of her high school, three years in succession as the 'High School Football Queen' and 'Future Farmers of America Queen.' She did not date too much, being extremely focussed on schoolwork. Unlike most of the other girls, including her cousin Alice and friend Margie, Cleo did not have her mind set on dating and marriage; she wanted to become a career girl. "When I attended Gonzalez High School I was voted football queen two years in a row and participated in many school plays. This all added fuel to my secret screen ambitions." As the 1940 school year ended and summer vacation began, the dancing and dating continued. That summer, a tragic automobile accident left the town of Gonzales in shock. Driving home from a day of shopping in Baton Rouge, pretty, vivacious, recent GHS graduate, Emeline Gautreau, was killed instantly in a one-car accident. Accompanying her were two of her sisters and three friends, who survived the horrible crash. The incident made a deep impact on Cleo and her schoolmates.

A happy event occurred when Murphy and Una became parents for the fourth time when their baby girl Jonnie Mae was born. The next year, Cleo graduated from Gonzales High School. The commencement exercises were held Thursday evening, April third at eight o'clock. At graduation, the boys wore suits and Cleo and the other girls wore long white evening dresses. The class colors that year were red and white and the girls carried a bouquet of their class flowers, red roses and fern. The gymnasium was used for graduation. That year's motto was, "A winner never quits, a quitter never wins." A motto Cleo embraced and focussed on in the years that yet were ahead of her. After graduation, Alice Causey married at sixteen and became pregnant soon afterwards. Margie Hodgeson romanced W. L.

6. *The Miami News*, March 7, 1955.

Diez, married him and would give birth to two sons. Cleo knew that this was not to be her path in life, at least not for the near future. She wanted to escape the harsh living circumstances in Louisiana.

After graduation, Cleo did get the opportunity to marry, too. Family doctor Gerald Louis Gaudin, who was ten years Cleo's senior, was charmed by the pretty girl. Dr. Gaudin had set up his practice in Gonzales in 1939.

GRADUATION PHOTO FROM GONZALES HIGH SCHOOL, CLEO STANDING IN THE SECOND ROW, SECOND FROM THE RIGHT, MARCH 1941.

He courted Cleo and asked for her hand. Cleo's parents thought she should take it seriously. Although Cleo was flattered by his attention, she declined the offer to become Mrs. Gaudin. Cleo's second Cousin Wendy Ortego remembers her mom, Betty Lee Causey, telling her that, "Doctor Gaudin was head over heels in love with Cleo. He had pictures of her all over his office. He never married because he was so much in love with her."[7]

In Cleo's last school year, her parents had bought a grocery store in Baton Rouge, the state capitol. They commuted back and forth to Galvez every day. At the insistence of Cleo, Murphy and Una decided to move to Baton Rouge. In the city, Cleo took a secretarial course at Pope's Commercial College and studied law. The young girl proved that she had a good business head. When she was eighteen, she did all the buying and

7. Source: email contact with author.

bookkeeping for her parents' store. For a while she forgot about her plans of going to Hollywood. Making money, and living a comfortable life was her focus for the near future. She concentrated on a job as a secretary. But her radiant beauty did not stay unnoticed. "I didn't think of pictures until everyone told me I was a ringer for Alice Faye, and ought to go to Hollywood."[8] That sparked the flame again and when she announced to her father that she would like to go to Hollywood, he decreed that she must either finish college or business school first. Cleo completed her two-year course at Pope's Commercial College in nine months. "And once again, I was so busy taking a short-cut to my diploma that there was very little time left for dates," she stated in a 1955 interview. Her statement was a little bit beside the truth.

At College she met and started dating late governor Huey Long's youngest son Palmer Reid. Palmer belonged to a prosperous family and although Cleo liked him a lot, the prospects of living in luxury for the rest of her life played a large part in the fact she gave the romance a chance. Becoming part of the Long family seemed a safe bet on a happy and easy life. But Palmer's mother didn't want her son to be associated with an ordinary working-class girl. She tried to prevent the two from seeing each other. Palmer was sent away from Louisiana for educational reasons and Mrs. Long hoped that would kill the romance. When Palmer spent the summer of 1941 in Los Angeles, attending the Anderson Aviation school, the lovebirds kept in touch. They wrote letters and promised each other eternal love, which was to be sealed by marriage as soon as he would return to Baton Rouge. Reluctantly, Mrs. Long had to give in to the two headstrong teenagers.

On Sunday, June 7, 1942, Cleo married twenty-one-year-old Palmer. She was eighteen. The ceremony was quietly performed before members of the two families and a few friends in Port Allen. The press was not invited and there were no pictures of the event in the newspapers. After the wedding ceremony the couple departed for a honeymoon in the West and on their return, they moved in with Palmer's mother at 305 Forrest Avenue, Shreveport. The wedding, although quietly solemnized, was of great interest throughout Louisiana and elsewhere. Mrs. Long was Louisiana's first woman U.S. Senator and the second woman in U.S. history ever elected Senator. After Huey P. Long was assassinated, she was appointed to fill his senate seat until a special election could be held three months later. She was elected to retain the seat in Congress and served until 1937. Cleo

8. *Hollywood Citizen News*, 1954.

looked up to Palmer's mother and she wondered if she, someday, could have a career in politics too.

Palmer and Cleo soon realized that they were not made to live the rest of their lives together. Besides, married life, although she had just experienced this reality for a couple of weeks, was not for Cleo. With all

that she had learned she felt useless just sitting around the house doing nothing. Palmer's mother had servants, Cleo was raised to work hard and do the household chores herself. She could not see herself as the typical Southern bourgeois married woman, sitting at home all day with her embroidery and drinking tea with her lady friends. Cleo realized that this was not the life that was meant for her. She had a hard time living in Mrs.

Long's household. She discussed the situation with her parents. They were opposed to the idea of a divorce, and Cleo had to do her best to convince them. After six weeks, the marriage was annulled. "We were too young. But we were just stubborn and wouldn't believe it when people told us that,"[9] Cleo commented later.[10]

During World War II, women filled in the jobs men had held before the war. African Americans and women, two groups historically denied

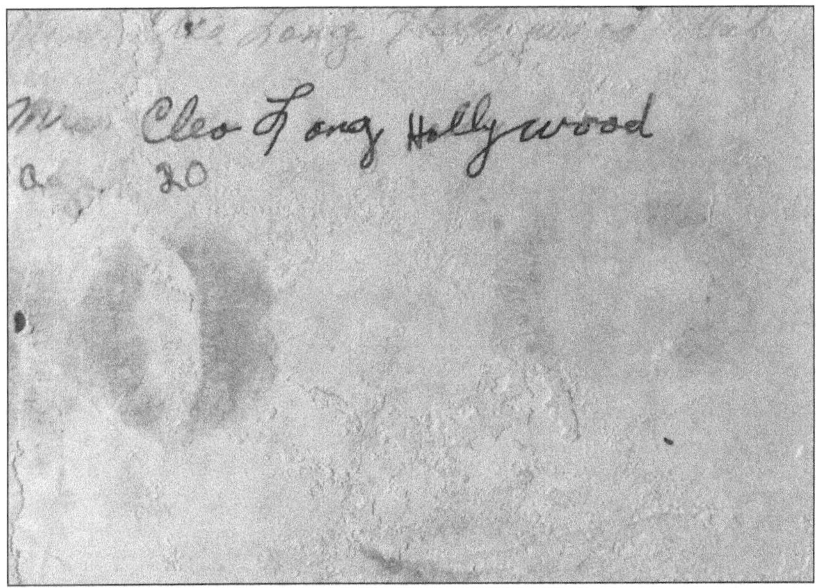

PREVIOUS PAGE, ABOVE: SIGNED PHOTO, MISS CLEO LONG HOLLYWOOD, 1944.

full access to many social and economic opportunities, now added to the wartime labor pool. After her divorce, Cleo worked at the Mengel Plant in Baton Rouge, where she built wooden ammunition boxes for the war. Cleo must have felt like "Rosie the Riveter," a well-known symbol for American women who worked in factories to support the war effort. Luckily for the family, Murphy Moore was not called for duty. With only daughters the family stayed intact, while other families missed their fathers and sons who were fighting overseas. In Louisiana there were more than thirty military

9. *Hollywood Citizen News*, 1954.

10. Wendy Ortego, daughter of Cleo's first cousin Betty Carter, told me that, "The Long family had their marriage annulled, because they thought that Cleo wasn't good enough for Palmer. When Cleo left for Hollywood, they wrote her a letter to help them with Palmer's political goals. She wrote them back and told them that, "if I wasn't good enough for you then, what makes you think I am good enough for you now." Needless to say, they never bothered her again."

installations. Army training camps trained soldiers for combat. As a result, the agriculture and industry grew. The increased demand for sugarcane, cotton and rice, helped the state's farmers recover from the economic devastation of the Great Depression. New Orleans remained the state's major industrial area, but Baton Rouge also served as an important industrial center. Civilians collected scraps, grew Victory gardens, and bought war

CLEO CIRCA 1945.

bonds to build aircraft. There were hundreds of servicemen, everywhere Cleo went. On her way home after work, they would walk beside her and ask her out, for an ice cream soda or a malt. Some of the girls Cleo worked with were getting pregnant. Very few were married, and Cleo felt sorry for them.

In her spare time, Cleo studied acting. Una and her friend Regina Hood talked about Cleo's talent and beauty and how this was wasted in Louisiana. Cleo confided in them that her childhood dream of becoming an actress was still in her heart. Regina encouraged Cleo, and persuaded Una and Murphy to do something with her beauty and intelligence. Baton Rouge was too small to develop her qualities, she advised Cleo to go to California to seek a career in Hollywood. Regina's daughter Melissa remembers, "Cleo was such an important person in my mother's life. Out here where we all live, everybody was pretty much friends. It was a small community but spread out over a large area. My mother taught Cleo and was instrumental in getting her to Hollywood. My mother was a teacher in Elementary School in Galvez. She started teaching there when she was fifteen and she became principal when she was seventeen. She went to, what was called, the Normal School. That was the name of the school that gave teacher's certificates. All the while she was buying property. She bought little pieces of property. And when she paid one off, she would buy another piece of property. My mother was a very smart businesswoman. Cleo was smart also. My mother saw Cleo's potential and thought that she belonged in Hollywood and was instrumental in getting her to leave and go to Hollywood. She saw her beauty, her intelligence, her dislike for the country life. Cleo wanted to be somebody. My mother saw that urge in her and she encouraged her to pursue her dream."[11]

HOLLYWOOD BOUND

Cleo's original plan was to go to New York and try for a part in a play soon after. Her parents were opposed to her plans to travel east. Murphy told his daughter that she was much too young to be on her own in such a big city. Cleo was determined to become an actress and she had pleaded with her parents to let her go to California instead. On June 21, 1944, the twenty-year-old girl arrived in Hollywood with a letter of recommendation to drama coach Josephine Dillon. She was determined to take acting and diction lessons with Clark Gable's first wife and worked hard to lose

11. Source: telephone conversation with author, 03-17-2020.

her southern drawl. "When I arrived in Hollywood, I had two strikes against me — being blonde and being from Dixie. A southern belle is supposed to have nothing else on her mind but romance, and if she's blond she isn't supposed to even have a mind."[12]

When Cleo returned to Louisiana to visit relatives, in the Summer of 1945, she had just made her first screen test for 20th Century-Fox. Dating

CLEO AND VICTOR MATURE AT THE TROCADERO, 1945.

Fox star Victor Mature had helped her to get in contact with the casting department at the studio. She visited family in Baton Rouge, Galvez and Gonzalez for two weeks, including her great-grandmother, Mrs. Jane Rheams, 101 years old, who resided on the outskirts of town. She captivated her family members with her stories about the stars she had met and told them that Fox talent scouts thought she resembled Alice Faye in looks and they had granted her a test. Cleo stayed at the Heidelberg Hotel in Baton Rouge. In the hotel lobby Cleo held a small press conference and told the reporters that she had formerly posed for magazine covers, done some modeling, and was currently studying dramatic acting under

12. *LA Daily News*, July 27, 1953.

Josephine Dillon. She mentioned that she had also appeared in two plays in Hollywood, *Personal Appearance* and *See Naples, and Die*.

Her old friends in Gonzales hosted several parties for her. One of the 'welcome home parties' was hosted by Regina Hood, her grammar schoolteacher. On Friday night, June 29, the Community of Galvez turned out en masse to welcome Cleo back, at the informal party in the Galvez grammar school. The gathering which overflowed the small room of the school building was completely captivated by the dynamic personality of Cleo. Mrs. Regina L. Hood introduced her to the group. She recalled how ambitious Cleo had been and told her that now she was close to realizing that ambition. Cleo paid tribute to Mrs. Hood who she said aided her in taking the first steps towards her goal. Cleo said that she had studied painting and tinting and had set up a studio in Baton Rouge, where she remained until she had saved enough money to go to Hollywood. Cleo mentioned the screen test for 20th Century-Fox and said she was anxious to go back to Hollywood to see the results. She hoped to get one of the major roles in a forthcoming picture. "My southern accent was my biggest handicap," she stated, but in her low, well-modulated speech was not a trace of that accent. She continued, "I know that I can be a success because you are all 'rooting' for me. I hope that I can make you as proud of me as I am of you." L. J. Babin, superintendent of schools in Ascension parish, lauded Cleo for her determination and will, "which shows that your future is unlimited…I wish you God-speed and success." Sheriff Lester Gonzales of Ascension parish told her that her charm and manner will assure success. Other representatives from Gonzales and Donaldsonville paid their tributes to Cleo and wished her success. After the talks, Cleo mingled with the crowd, renewing acquaintances, and signed autographs for all her admirers. Refreshments were served and entertainment was furnished by Bruce Broussard and his Round-Up Boys. [13]

Back in Hollywood Cleo learned that her screen test was not resulting in a contract. Although Alice Faye had left the studio after filming *Fallen Angel* (1945), because she was disappointed many of her best scenes were cut, Fox executives didn't see the need to replace her. They were already grooming June Haver for stardom and the studio earned a lot of money with their musical star Betty Grable.

Being from Louisiana, coming to Hollywood was like entering a fantasy land. Having dreamed of going to Hollywood her entire youth, seeing where the pictures were really made, visiting the sound stages and meeting

13. *Advocate*, Baton Rouge, La., Sat., June 30, 1945.

EARLY PUBLICITY PHOTO, 1945.

the people who made the pictures, was a dream come true. After being out in Hollywood for a couple of months, Cleo returned to Louisiana in her beaten-up old car. She picked up her mother, sisters, dog and cat, and moved them with her to California. Murphy stayed in Baton Rouge; he wrapped up his business and followed his wife and daughters to start a new life in the West. "My parents came to Hollywood with me, certain that my burning ambition would pass as soon as I discovered what a tough nut Hollywood was to crack. But when they found they had a very determined daughter on their hands, we all went back to Louisiana, sold our property, and returned to live here permanently."[14]

"Cleo's parents were like salt of the earth people," Melissa Hood Duhe recalls. "Very unassuming, unpretentious. It seemed that they didn't particularly like California. It was not Galvez and Murphy couldn't plant his crops. In Galvez everybody had acres and acres of property and they didn't in California."[15] The family had made a huge sacrifice leaving everything behind. Although Una missed her relatives and friends, she and Murphy put their focus on building up a new life with their children. Murphy started his building company. Cleo focused on her acting career and helped her dad in his business. Although her father had his doubts, she told him not to worry, promising that one day she would own the town, and she was going to be a movie star, too. Murphy Moore remembered years later, "I thought the child was a little tetched in the head. But by gum, she's seen it through."[16] Una was also apprehensive about it. Deep in her heart Cleo's religious mother was not happy with the career decision her daughter had made, but she supported her choice. "When she was five years old, she came to me and told me she wanted to be an actress. Ever since she has been obsessed with that idea. My husband and I tried our best to realize her dreams, Murphy even found work here in California. I must admit that Cleo has proven herself as a loving daughter and she is appreciative for the things we have done for her. She is a sweet girl and always attentive towards others. Whenever possible she will join us in going to church and is always willing to help around with charity work for our church organization. But sometimes I worry about the fact that Cleo lets her heart rule her head. On the other hand, if she would be any different, she probably wouldn't be a daughter of mine."[17]

14. *Hollywood Stars*, 1955.

15. Source: telephone interview with author, 03-17-2020.

16. *San Bernardino Sun*, July 8, 1956.

17. *Piccolo*, December 1955.

Never at any point did Una or Murphy try to set their foot down, telling Cleo that "She can't do it." They were helpful and hopeful through every step of the process. Cleo's teenage sister Yvonne wasn't enthusiastic about her parents' decision to help further her sister's career. She was forced to leave her friends behind in Louisiana. But Yvonne was not the type to complain, she just adjusted herself to the new situation. One of Cleo's nephews underlines, "Yvonne was quite introverted, very shy indeed. At a party she would be the one sitting in the corner just watching people. She was not one to initiate conversation. Cleo was the sister that craved attention when she was younger."[18]

The family settled in Tarzana, a suburban neighborhood in the San Fernando Valley region of Los Angeles, where they rented a bungalow. Murphy had sold the grocery store. They purchased enough stables to stock the family larder for a few weeks. Said Cleo, "When I arrived in Hollywood, the first thing I did was spend $75 on groceries and stock food under the bed and in the closet — I was that scared I might starve. I also studied the real-estate business in case I couldn't make the grade as an actress."[19] "I once read somewhere a long time ago that when Marie Wilson first hit Hollywood, she did the same thing. I figured this was a pretty smart idea, but I didn't waste any time looking for a job."[20]

Over the years, the Moore's stayed close with their relatives and friends in the South. Cleo and her parents never forgot those who were part of their life before they left for California. Melissa Hood Duhe remembers the many times Cleo returned to Galvez. "She was so loving and kind and sweet. It was sort of indescribable the way she felt about her family here and those people who loved her here. She was just a very, very kind person. She was the epitome of loveliness. I can't tell you what she was like when she would come to these community gatherings they would have when she would come home. She acted like she was the one that was so enamoured by the people here. Everybody here just thought we were thrilled to death by Cleo come to visit us, and she was feeling the same way, to have us to come home to. Everybody was hugging her and kissing her and there was just a bunch of very angry women, cause all the men were just drawn to her like a magnet. She was beautiful."[21] The encouragement and love she received every time she returned to

18. Source: email contact with author.

19. *Toledo Blade*, September 5, 1954.

20. *LA Daily News*, July 27, 1953.

21. Source: telephone conversation with author, 03-17-2020.

CLEO CIRCA 1945.

Louisiana helped her to keep pursuing her dream of becoming a world-famous movie star.

Alice Causey's son Luther Jerry Diez recalls, "Cleo came out every year, to my house. A lot of the neighbors would gather, out of curiosity. Cleo would visit with us and hang out. When my daddy was in service, I was a real young kid, he was stationed in San Diego during World War II. We stayed with Cleo and her family for months."[22] On September 2, 1945, World War II came to an end. America's involvement in the war had a significant impact on the economy. Driven by growing consumer demand, as well as the continuing expansion of the military-industrial complex as the Cold war ramped up, the United States reached new heights of prosperity in the years after the war.

With the family firmly settled and the larder restocked, Cleo and her dad bought a couple of lots in Tarzana. They planned to build and sell bungalows. Cleo discussed with her father how profitable their endeavor would be and she unfolded her plans to expand their business. In the years after WWII, the unemployment rate in California was higher than in the rest of the United States. Most of the war veterans hoped for a speedy return to a civilian life, some of them deciding to stay on in the Golden State hoping to find new opportunities. Besides jobs there was also a shortage in houses for the young married couples. A baby boom was foreseen. Murphy also realized how lucrative the construction business was and he decided to build two bungalows. When the bungalows were completed and sold, half of the money was put in the bank, and four more lots were bought with the other half. "The $2,000 daddy got for the store was our whole bankroll. When we arrived here, it was right after the war and there was a housing shortage, so I went to a real-estate agent. He had some land for sale with a house on it for $16,000. I asked him real nice if he'd take $2,000 down. He agreed, so I put daddy to work — he's a wonderful carpenter — fixing the house. The rest of us put in a lawn and painted and did everything. Less than two months later I sold the house for $18,000. I divided the rest of the land into six lots and sold them off at $6,500 each."[23]

Hollywood had provided distraction from everyday life and sorrow during the war. The demand for new movies and movie stars grew. Cleo was ready and eager to crash the movie studio gates again, but she was smart enough to see that the whole town was loaded with well-built wannabe actresses. So, aware of what she had to sell, she dieted and exercised

22. Source: telephone conversation with author.

23. *Parade*, July 8, 1956.

to lose weight, and scouted for commercial modelling jobs. Within weeks, she was doing seven or eight photo sittings weekly, at $25 per photo shoot. The blonde beauty showed she had brains and she planned a campaign. She entered beauty contests, picking ones where the competition was not too hard, and ultimately was named Miss Van Nuys for 1948. Most of the other beauty titles were meaningless, but they helped her to gain attention.

CLEO CIRCA 1946.

Before she was crowned Miss Van Nuys, she was queen of the Van Nuys Rotary club. Being Miss Van Nuys gained a lot of publicity. Her pictures were featured regularly in the newspapers when she attended a luncheon, opened a store or was seen at a parade. One of her first assignments was welcoming the round-the-world-fliers George W. Truman and Clifford V. Evans at Van Nuys Metropolitan Airport on November 26. The fliers

MISS VAN NUYS GREETS GEORGE W. TRUMAN AND CLIFFORD V. EVANS, NOVEMBER 1947.

were greeted by more than 1,000 people. Cleo posed for the battery of photographers representing newspapers and wire services. The event was broadcast by two national networks.

While Cleo focussed on a career in show business, Cleo's 17-year-old sister got engaged. Cleo and her family attended the wedding of Yvonne and William Denis Saunders on February 15, in Los Angeles. Unlike Cleo, Yvonne was focussed on married life and raising children. She was quite happy to be the housewife and mother in the background. Yvonne followed Cleo's career closely, quite happy to live vicariously through her. In fact, she was to become the President of the Cleo Moore fan club, answering letters and mailing pictures. "The entire "sisterhood" was very close. Until they moved from the Valley, the entire family would have Sunday dinner together. Of course not everyone would be there every Sunday but most of the time, yes. Yvonne and Cleo were particularly close, probably because they were the closest in age. Marilea was a true intellectual, incredibly smart and as such was a bit standoffish," one of Cleo's nephews recalls. "She was the only college graduate of the sisters. As I got older, we enjoyed spending time together, especially as I planned to go to UCLA also. Jonnie Mae was always the little sister, much younger than her sisters. My grandparents, the grandchildren called them Nana and Papa, were awesome. True 'salt of the earth' folks. Both my grandparents were quiet and soft spoken, but Papa especially was a man of few words. However, when he spoke, you'd better listen. In the summers I would spend many weekends, even whole weeks with them on 'the hill' in Tarzana. That's what we all called their custom-built house. I also spent a lot of time there with Jonnie Mae who was still living at home; she was in her teens, as she was just ten years older than me."[24]

On February 18, Cleo participated in the "Welcome Chevrolet" parade, to celebrate the opening of a huge new Chevrolet assembly plant in the San Fernando Valley. Republic Pictures western star 'Wild Bill' Elliott, four elephants from Bailey Brothers' circus, 'Miss Chevrolet' Joan Wallace and the Los Angeles Police band were some of the others who participated in the parade. Directly after she was crowned Miss Van Nuys, Cleo got a contract offer from Warner Brothers. Although the salary was less than she had been receiving as a freelance model, Cleo saw it as the chance she had been waiting for and signed. With her contract, she was permitted onto sound stages, and she felt like she was entering a whole new world. From dawn till dusk, she saw actors rehearsing, electricians, set builders and camera people hurrying around. Cleo was ready and willing to participate in it all. Six months went by, but no film roles were offered to her. However, the studio did keep her busy posing for cheesecake art. Finally, in April 1948, she was cast for a small part in *Embraceable You* (1948). Realizing Warners' was not intending to invest in her career, Cleo asked for a release and got it.

Now that she had one foot in the door, she sent out her headshots and pin-up photos to casting agencies, talent scouts and all the film studios. She was notified that Columbia was looking for a leading lady for one of their new serials. A screen test was arranged, and Cleo won the part of Ruth Culver, the heiress of a fortune who is sought after by Congo Bill (Don McGuire). "Working in that film was a big encouragement.

24. Source: email contact with author.

Everyone was so helpful. I forgot that most producers were thinking of me as a poster ad instead of an actress."[25] Although the filming was challenging, Cleo loved every minute of it. About the making of *Congo Bill* Cleo later recalled, "It was a serial. When I walked on that sound stage, I was really scared to death. The big lights and the camera scared me I guess. I thought they just used a small Brownie camera. It was a jungle picture.

SIGNED PHOTOGRAPH FOR REGINA HOOD, CIRCA 1946.

I had no stand-in or double, and it was an experience I will never forget. I had to jump from trees, get caught in quicksand and sink to my neck. I was screaming for real, and the director thought it was acting and kept saying, 'Sensational.' When I got home I was just black and blue. But for this I was receiving $150 a week."[26]

On the Columbia studio lot she met another young hopeful. Marilyn Monroe had been signed by Harry Cohn to star in *Ladies of the Chorus*, for which filming had started in April. Cleo arrived at the studio that same month. Both starlets were given the chance to star in a B-movie production and they hoped that this opportunity would lead to bigger

25. *Morning Advocate,* June 1, 1952.

26. Toledo Blade, September 5, 1954.

PUBLICITY PHOTO, CIRCA 1947.

roles at the studio that was reigned by Rita Hayworth. But that was wishful thinking. Both Marilyn and Cleo were let go after their one movie. Cleo's days at Columbia lasted slightly longer. The *Congo Bill* chapters were filmed between April and September. The following Autumn and Winter, Cleo picked up working with her father and returned to Baton Rouge regularly for two-week visits. On September 26, Cleo celebrated the one-hundred-and-third birthday of her great-grandmother, Mrs. Jane McCrory-Rheams of Hope Villa. With her to celebrate were seven of her children, three already died, 21 grandchildren and 50 great-grandchildren and three great-great-grandchildren.[27]

On October 28, the first chapter of *Congo Bill* was released. A newspaper article mentioned Cleo and it endorsed her film star potential. "Serials have served as a springboard to fame for many film stars, both male and female, and producer Sam Katzman, recognized as Hollywood's serial king, is of the opinion that Cleo Moore, beautiful blond leading lady of his latest Columbia chapter-thriller, "Congo Bill," will become another motion picture celebrity as a result of her portrayal."[28]

Another promising career opportunity came in the form of an offer from former MGM producer Al Lewis, who had formed a production company with novelist Edward Thompson. In October Cleo signed a five-year contract, starting with a $500 a week salary that would increase to $2500 a week in the last year of the contract. Lewis and Thompson planned to film five novels of the latter, starting with one in February 1949. Cleo was over the moon to be signed to star in *Take Away the Darkness*. When the two men could not come up with enough financial backing, the deal fell through. Cleo swallowed her frustration and moved on to other things. She concluded her year of being Miss Van Nuys by taking part in the Christmas parade on December 10. She attracted press through her pin-up and modeling work, severing a tire chain to open a new Pep Boys store in Van Nuys, and posing in the sensuous 'Riviera Peasant Blouse.' She was heralded 'Miss Plastic Art,' posing in a costume, in which everything was made entirely of plastic, from the orchid in her hair to her gloves, to illustrate the variety of plastic arts that were displayed at the California Hobby Show on May 27, 1949. Cleo enjoyed the attention she garnered, but most of all she wanted to act and further her film career. When Cleo knocked on the door of Warner Bros. Studios, they took her in on a one-year-contract.

27. Mrs. Jane McCrory-Rheams died May 22, 1951, 105 years old.

28. *The Cincinnati Enquirer*, January 16, 1949.

Cleo's nights on the town with various men provided copy for Hollywood columnists. During 1949 Al Mathes is her steady date and — according to the press — a serious candidate for marriage. Mathes was a tough Boyle Heights street kid who became a well-known Hollywood and Beverly Hills restaurateur and gambler. Cleo admired Mathes for what he achieved, in a way she recognized herself in him. Raised in poverty, they

both worked hard to make their life more comfortable. The relationship ended, because Cleo was not willing to give up her career for a romance, let alone marriage. She had plans for her future and was not willing to let a man pay her way. She wanted to earn it herself.

After a couple of bit parts, Warner Bros. decided not to renew her contract. The studio had set its eyes on blonde Barbara Payton. They decided she was to be the starlet they wanted to groom for stardom. Barbara Payton

RKO STUDIOS PUBLICITY PHOTO, 1950.

was a beautiful and talented blonde. She loved to play the field and ruined her career chances because she garnered too much negative publicity in the one year she was under contract. Cleo took notice and learned that a good girl earns praise, but a bad girl earns publicity. For a starlet this was a thin line to walk. Cleo needed all the publicity she could get without being shamed and blamed. She had achieved some success in Hollywood, but she had little to no acting experience. Two years later, she recalled how she viewed her chances when she was a struggling starlet. "When I came from Louisiana for a visit four years ago, I believed that a girl couldn't get into films without several years of acting experience. Then I found out that nature can provide one with an entry. Later I discovered, however, that nature's contribution doesn't necessarily prolong a girl's stay in the movies. You must learn to act, too."[29] Cleo was becoming pretty sick of posing in bathing suits, with a Halloween pumpkin or Thanksgiving turkey. She wanted to get away from the still cameras and before the motion picture kind.

An ardent boxing fan, Cleo visited the matches at the Hollywood Legion Stadium regularly. It was there that an RKO talent scout saw her and asked her to come over for a screen test. A meeting with director of casting, Bill White, was arranged and she was sent to dramatic coach Lillian Albertson. Albertson saw the potential in her and as a result Cleo was rushed into a total of six films at RKO. She scarcely had time to take a breath between filming, except, of course, before a still camera for that same old cheesecake buildup. Her best performance from the RKO period was in director Nicholas Ray's *On Dangerous Ground* (1951), a film noir classic. "My first real part was in *On Dangerous Ground*. A small part, with Ida Lupino and Bob Ryan in the leads. I was thrilled and really impressed, because Ida Lupino and I were the only girls in the picture."[30] Cleo reported to the soundstage on August 7, 1950. After being completed, the film was shelved for more than a year, which was not uncommon at RKO. The press took notice of the new girl at RKO and they published her photos, but that didn't lead to starring roles. When her contract ended, she started making the rounds at various studios again. One of the studios was 20th Century-Fox. A year earlier they had considered her for the role of Miss Caswell in *All About Eve* (1950). Of course, 20th Century-Fox executives judged otherwise. Marilyn Monroe, who was also tested, won the part.

29. *LA Times*, November 2, 1952.

30. *Piccolo*, December 1955.

Sidney Skolsky, show business reporter, witnessed Cleo's screen test and was impressed. He wrote, "I had just walked on the Fox lot when a messenger boy approached me. Looking around, as if the FBI might be lurking nearby, he whispered, "Get a load of what they're shooting on the Test Stage!" And he vanished. I hurried over. The Test Stage was packed — standing room only. Jerry Webb, the test director, said, "I've been shoot-

CLEO WITH CIRO'S DISC JOCKEY, JOHNNY GRANT. APRIL 1950.

ing tests for years and I've never had a crowd like this. Word gets around, doesn't it?" "What's the attraction?" I asked. Webb didn't have to answer; into the bedroom set walked a bosomy blonde wearing a transparent black nightgown. She made Jane Russell look anaemic, and there's no telling what she would have done to the Johnston Office. "I'm just making a routine test of a girl," explained Webb, "Her name is Cleo Moore. I think

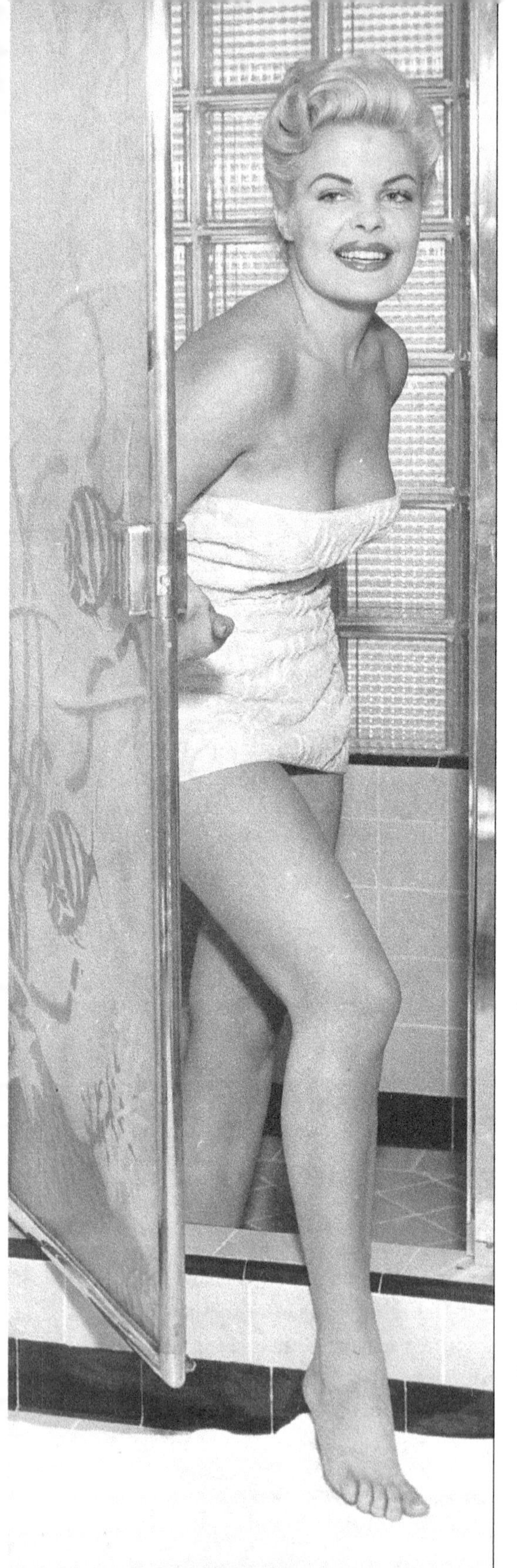

Georgie Jessel discovered her. We want to see if she's got anything. Cleo stood there in her nightgown and also wore a broad smile. She realized she had attracted a record crowd and was enjoying it. After all, Cleo was trying to sell herself and land a movie contract. "Usually it takes an hour or so to shoot a test," explained Webb. "We've been here all day." Electricians were still adjusting lights. "Is it getting hot?" asked Webb. "Who are you talking to?" Cleo asked. She got a bigger laugh than any comic on TV. "I mean you, honey," said Webb. "I want you to be comfortable." It was the first time Cleo had spoken. I looked at her face. She resembled Alice Faye, but only in looks. I guess the best way to describe her is to say, "Petty Girl." If they had used Cleo Moore in that story, they wouldn't have needed a story, which they didn't have. "Okay, honey," said Webb, "we're ready. I want you to walk into the boudoir, lean on the chaise-longue, and start talking. Don't be nervous. You're safer here than in your own bedroom. Webb gave the signal. The camera started turning. Cleo Moore followed herself into the boudoir as the pianist on the set pounded out "That Old Black Magic." Cleo looked straight into the camera and spoke her lines: "Hello. I'm glad to meet you. I'm

Cleo Moore…blonde…blue eyes…height, five feet four…weight, 112… bust, oh, that isn't important…" She read that line well. I'm willing to make a bet that she gets the job. You'll be seeing her."[31]

Cleo's screen test didn't lead to a contract. Marilyn Monroe was signed by Fox in December. Disappointed but not defeated, Cleo showed herself serious about her career and worked hard to improve her acting skills. Next to occasional modelling assignments she took acting, diction, singing and dancing classes.

HUGO HAAS' MUSE

Cleo's big opportunity came in the form of Hugo Haas. The Czechoslovakian-born actor-writer-producer-director had just turned out a whopping success for Columbia in *Pick-Up*. He made one more movie with its star, Beverly Michaels, before she accepted a contract offer from Universal-International. Haas started a search for a leading lady for his new production. Louella Parsons reports in her newspaper column that, "Flame-haired Zsa Zsa Gabor, one of the noted Gabor sisters and the wife of George Sanders, has been signed by Hugo Haas to make a picture. The story is a very dramatic one called *Thy Neighbor's Wife*. In it she will play the young wife of a judge (Hugo Haas). It's a bad marriage, and when she's out with her lover, his uncle is killed and the young man is blamed for the murder. He cannot give an alibi. The judge who tries the case is the wronged husband, and, oh, well, there's a lot more to it — another murder and heavy drama. Haas doesn't make conventional pictures ever."[32] But Zsa Zsa got a better deal at MGM and backed off.

Haas tested several actresses including blonde starlet Gloria Pall. "I met Hugo Haas and he wanted to sign me. The resemblance between Cleo and myself was uncanny. She was a short version of me. He had Beverly Michaels at the time. She was my height. They normally sign short or average height gals. Hugo Haas wanted to sign me up but then everyone said I was a king-size version of Cleo Moore."[33] When Haas met Cleo, he was immediately taken by her appearance. Cleo recalled about her first meeting with Hugo, "Then someone told me that Hugo Haas was looking for a girl of my type for *Thy Neighbor's Wife*. I telephoned his secretary and asked

31. *New York Post*, September 21, 1950.

32. *Rochester Democrat and Chronicle*, June 9, 1951.

33. Source: email contact with author.

for an appointment." A meeting was scheduled, and Hugo liked what he saw. "He took one look at me and said, "You look the part. Now if you only can act a little!' He made a test and, well, I guess I did it all right."[34] Cleo agreed to take the proposal of working for free in exchange for a share in the picture. Haas also offered to sign her to a five-picture contract.

Filming started in the Summer of 1951, on an eleven-day schedule. With the profits from his huge success *Pickup*, and its successor *Girl on the*

ABOVE: CLEO VISITS TOM CRACRAFT, HEAD SCENIC ARTIST OF COLUMBIA PICTURES, MAY 1952. LEFT: PUBLICITY PHOTO FOR *ONE GIRL'S CONFESSION*, WITH HUGO HAAS.

Bridge, Haas invested in what he wanted to be his best film. Costs reached an estimate $100,000. Elaborate sets, beautiful costumes and period settings make *Thy Neighbor's Wife* very enjoyable to watch. Although not listed as an A-movie, it's unfair to call this film a B-movie. It's got the quality and atmosphere of a European movie, especially a German film from the 1930s or 1940s. The close-ups of Cleo emphasize that feeling. Cleo looks gorgeous and the close-ups of her strong facial expressions show her ability as an actress.

When finished, *Thy Neighbor's Wife* failed to find a distributor. But Hugo Haas kept his word to star Cleo in his next production. In February

34. *LA Examiner*, July 19, 1953.

1952, they started to rehearse for *Strange Fascination*. Louella Parsons wrote a sympathetic article in her syndicated column, "Right now Cleo Moore may not be one of the best-known actresses in Hollywood, but she is one of the most ambitious, and that's for sure. Cleo, who is not unlike Rita Hayworth in face and streamlining, has just finished some heavy emoting in Hugo Haas's *Thy Neighbor's Wife*, and she is signed for two more Haas films. *Strange Fascination* is the first, and the other will be made in Italy."[35] The Italian production was never made. *Strange Fascination* tells the story of a sexy blonde dancer who becomes the obsession of a famous pianist. Their romance eventually destroys him and his career. In real life, Cleo and Hugo had become romantically involved too. It had happened when they were working on *Thy Neighbor's Wife*. Cleo adored Hugo and was thankful for giving her a chance to star in his movies. She showed her gratitude when rehearsing for her next picture at Haas's house.

Haas trusted on Cleo's dramatic acting ability and giving her top billing above himself. This hastened Cleo to remark, "I've never been so thrilled in my life. I also have an exotic tango routine, so all my years of dance lessons are going to count. Let the stills fall where they may. I'm a motion picture actress at last."[36]

On March 19, the cameras started rolling on the set of *Strange Fascination*. One day actress Beverly Michaels visited the set and met her successor. There is a picture capturing the moment, with Haas standing between Beverly and Cleo. Beverly and Hugo are all smiles, but Cleo looks as if she wants to be someplace else. Actress Karen Sharpe was just starting her career when Haas cast her for a small part in the movie. Karen mentions, "Beverly might have visited the set when I was working, but you know I was very concentrated on what I was doing. I was not used to having to hit the marks on the floor and I never worked in front of a camera before and so I had a lot on my mind. I didn't want to make any mistakes. And if she did visit the set, nobody was really excited about it or about anything. You know, we shot so quickly in those days." She added, "I didn't really have any scenes with Cleo Moore. Filming the movie was a very lovely experience. I enjoyed it and I loved Hugo Haas. He was very professional. He was very nice to me. I understand that he and Cleo were having an affair, but I never saw that."[37]

35. January 2, 1952.

36. *Advocate*, June 1, 1952.

37. Source: telephone interview with author, 06-04-2016.

Jan Lowell was billed as Jan Englund and played small parts in several of Haas's movies. Jan's husband Mark was the dialogue supervisor on many of Haas's productions. Jan and Mark Lowell also knew of the liaison. "As for the affair between Hugo and Cleo we all knew, it was no secret, although we all pretended it was," Jan remembers. "Hugo and Bibi had a great marriage, had been through hell together [during the Nazi

CLEO WITH HER ARTWORK, 1952.

occupation of their country] and their love for each other was based on so much more than sex that neither to my knowledge talked about the affair."[38]

In May, Hugo's wife Bibi obtained a divorce in Superior Court, even though she wasn't on hand to testify. She was in a hospital bed in Milan, Italy. She made her plea for freedom by deposition. The former actress and dancer, known professionally in Europe under the name of Maria De Bibikoff, charged Hugo with cruelty, including the use of vile language against her in the presence of their thirteen-year-old son Ivan. The court was told that Bibi became ill in Italy during a trip she took following their stormy separation in October. The couple had separated earlier in 1952, when Bibi found out about the affair of her husband with Cleo. She immediately left their home at 1542 N. Orange Grove Avenue in Los Angeles and took her son Ivan with her. The couple's property settlement involved joint custody of their son and a $2000 monthly alimony for Bibi. She also received $5500 for a share in their home. Haas hinted towards the affair with Cleo years later, when he said, "The young girl-elderly man theme has fascinated me since the famous Emil Jannings films; besides, there might be a little bit of my own problems involved."[39]

Because of the three-picture deal Hugo had with Columbia Pictures they distributed his upcoming movie, *Story of a Bad Girl*. The actors started rehearsing late July and actual filming started August 18. Re-titled *One Girl's Confession*, it shows Cleo as a waitress who steals back the money that her boss stole from her father. She confesses to her crime, serves time in prison and comes out a reformed girl.

After the success of *Strange Fascination*, Cleo's nickname as the 'Bad Blonde of the B-movies' was established with *One Girl's Confession*. The movie exhibitors and the public wanted to see more of Cleo Moore. 20th Century-Fox heard the cry and Hugo was asked to show *Thy Neighbor's Wife*. They bought the rights to the movie and distributed the movie in September 1953. At that time, the studio was grooming Marilyn Monroe for stardom. In January, her movie *Niagara* had been released, and she was filming *Gentlemen Prefer Blondes*, to be released in August. Haas negotiated that he could film another picture with Cleo at the studio.

Cleo, keen on being clashed with Marilyn, wanted to paint the billboard for *Thy Neighbor's Wife* herself. Marilyn had made headlines with

<hr>

38. Source: mail contact with author. Lowell: "Proof is that even after their divorce Bibi, who then lived half time in Italy, would return to California and move back in the house, take over, cook, have parties etc. And Hugo was always thrilled she was returning. Eventually they got back together again, moved to NYC, then Rome Italy, then Vienna, where Hugo died."

39. *Films in Review*, February 1978.

her nude calendar photos and saw her popularity rise because of it. Cleo wanted to step on the bandwagon, too. She made public that she painted the poster for one reason: "The studio's version might not be curvy enough. When the studio does posters, they draw them from photographs and the artist doesn't know you. He does a flat surface. It isn't three-dimensional. The last poster made me look like Jean Harlow, not like me at all."[40] For the

ONE GIRL'S CONFESSION, 1953.

poster, Cleo posed herself nude from the waist up with a long braid of her blonde hair in a strategic place. She got her inspiration from a particular scene in the movie. "In the picture, I hang from a cross with my blouse torn half off. I am being punished by the villagers for adultery."[41] The result proved to be good publicity, but too daring for the studio. So, Cleo painted another version that was used for theatrical release.

At the time, Cleo's biggest frustration was the constant comparison to Marilyn Monroe. Sidney Skolsky had mentioned in his column 'That's Hollywood for You,' that "…they're saying Cleo Moore is another Marilyn

40. *The Times-News*, January 31, 1953.

41. The actual scene Cleo mentions is not seen in the final cut of the movie. There is a still depicting the scene she describes.

Monroe."[42] Dorothy Manners headlined a newspaper article, 'Curvaceous Cleo Moore 'Answer' to Monroe.' She wrote, "If all the studios' 'answers' to Marilyn Monroe were set — er — side by side they'd be quite a production. Columbia's entry in the field of What's-Marilyn-Got-That-Our-Girl-Hasn't-Got is a luscious, big-eyed blonde from New Orleans, named Cleo Moore."[43] Cleo hated being referred to as 'another Marilyn.' She resented the fact that she would always come in second base, with Marilyn winning the match. She kept working on her acting skills and focused on her career in show business, telling herself that there was room enough for another sexy blonde leading lady. Occasionally Cleo would comment on her comparison to Marilyn. "We started out at the same time. We auditioned for the same parts. I needed the opportunity and a chance and so did she. Well, she won of course. They had to make a choice and Marilyn won. Years ago, we were the best of friends, but we don't see each other that often anymore, which is a shame."[44]

Show business is a competitive business. Cleo liked to compete, her desires and ambitions steered her life and had brought her to Hollywood. In high school she'd worked hard to be the best student but competing with other beautiful starlets over a job acquired other skills. She felt her acting skills were downgraded to her physical appearance. For that goal Cleo had to work hard to keep in shape physically; telling herself how superficial that side of her career was. Apart from a career as a movie star, Cleo ambitioned a career in politics. Working for the people, their welfare had been installed in her since a young age. In May 1953, she stood as a candidate for honorary mayor of her hometown Tarzana. In the 1930s, '40s and '50s, celebrities entered the political arena, some to support candidates, some to raise their fading glory, and others because they truly hoped to provide public service. Many Hollywood stars served as honorary mayors in their communities, bringing recognition to their local neighborhoods and advocating for public services, roads and parks to better people's lives. The voting ballot shows that Cleo was the only woman in this election. Competing with her were actors Pat Knowles and Garry Goodwin. When the polls closed at six p.m. on May 26, Cleo was not a winner. Cleo knew that being a woman, she had to work harder than any other to get what she wanted. Her parents had once called her headstrong; for Cleo there was no mountain too high to climb, no obstacles could deter her path.

42. *Photoplay*, December 1952.

43. *LA Examiner*, April 19, 1953.

44. *Piccolo*, November 1955.

On July 16, Cleo, visited Louisiana for a short vacation. She was the featured guest at a luncheon given by Mrs. Hood in Donaldsville. Cleo attended the luncheon with her mother. A corsage was given her by Mrs. Upton Dugas and Mrs. N. J. Hidalgo, local florists. Among the luncheon guests was Mayor Sidney A. Marchand Jr., who presented her with the original key to the Gonzales city hall. Cleo also visited her uncle,

CLEO POSING WITH STUYVESANT AT WHEELING DOWNS, MARCH 1953.

A.C. Palmer, before returning to California after an exhaustive personal appearance tour. It was her first trip to home environs in four years, and she was so impressed she said she would go back a year from Christmas. "Columbia said my tour was the most successful any of its stars have taken, including Rita Hayworth," Cleo told the press. Her itinerary included three shows a day at most theatres. "I just talk. I tell women in the early

1953 BALLOT FOR HONORARY MAYOR OF TARZANA, CALIFORNIA.

show things like how movies are made and makeup and beauty hints. For the little gangsters at the night show I tell be-bop jokes." On one of her visits back home, Cleo took Hugo Haas with her. Connie Ray Hodgeson remembers that "She came back home, and we had a gathering. We had a good time. She brought her agent with her and they spend the day with hugging and kissing. When I was in Korea, they put her picture on the airplane."[45]

In the Summer of 1953 Haas starts shooting his new production with Cleo and John Agar. *Bait* tells the story of two gold miners who are set up against each other once a beautiful girl comes to live with them. Unlike what the poster and publicity taglines might suggest, Cleo's character is a vulnerable girl, hurt by the lies and peoples' judgements. "She's the

45. Source: telephone conversation with author.

bait in a man-trap," the posters screamed. A mantrap that is set by Haas, who has married her just so he can catch her alone with John Agar, his partner. His plan is to kill both, thereby keeping all the gold for himself. While they were rehearsing, Haas asked Cleo to put in mind the shame and sorrow of a girl that had become an outcast, because she had a baby out of wedlock. Cleo could relate to that on some level, remembering the unlucky girls who got pregnant in high school. Haas talked with her about his ordeals, being a Jew in Czechoslovakia in WW II. He was a deeply traumatized man, who had lost his parents and brother and other relatives in the Holocaust. He told Cleo he used his movies to cope with his feelings of loss, pain, and dispossession. Haas's films were strongly informed by his survivor guilt and trauma. Cleo listened and felt even more attached to him. Although the romance was coming to an end, Cleo respected Haas and out of that respect grew a warm and generous friendship.

Bait was much publicized, using Cleo's daring bathtub scene. Cleo wanted to paint the poster for this movie too, but her version with the bathing scene was not printed. To keep the focus on her daring scenes she fed the press with her witty remarks. They asked her what would happen when these portions were cut out. Cleo answered, "If they are deleted, it would be a very short movie." Her pin-up persona, wise-cracking remarks and ability to spot a good gimmick, became the trademark of the nick-named 'Canary Blonde Bombshell from Louisiana.' Interested in other aspects of film making, Cleo reportedly told the press that she intended to produce a movie herself. "Lately, I have taken more than passing interest, plus some notes, on the production end of the business. I'm searching now for a good script and may get going before long." She added, "Making pictures looks no more difficult than making houses."[46]

Gossip-columnist Hedda Hopper mentions that Cleo is a talented girl that Hollywood had not yet discovered. She predicted that Cleo would hit fame in the movie capitol in the year to come. Hopper's prediction proved to be right. Producer Leonard Goldstein, the steady date of Universal starlet Piper Laurie, signed Cleo to a long-term contract in January. Goldstein had set up his own production company and he announced Cleo as the star in the re-make of his production *The Desert Hawk* (1950), to be titled *Hawk of the Desert*.

On January 18 of the new year Cleo attended the welcome back party for actress Terry Moore who had returned from Korea, where she had entertained the soldiers who were stationed there. Darryl F. Zanuck,

46. *Times Daily*, September 16, 1953.

head of 20th Century-Fox, threw an Oriental party at Ciro's night club. Cleo won the honors for the lowest neckline. The next month Cleo left Hollywood for a publicity tour for her picture *Bait*. A newspaper review mentioned, "Haas, who does pretty well as the prospector, presents his story without clutter. This is a one-track tale and he sticks close to it — extraneous details are not permitted to intrude. Most of the action is

CLEO WITH LANCE FULLER, JANUARY 1954.

limited to Miss Moore's climbing into and out of her bunk bed, slapping a little food on the table and puttering at the sink, while the men sit around eyeing her, or stamp off into the snow scene visible from the window and stamp back again, with snow on their shoulders. Curiously, this meagre set-up does engender a kind of emotional excitement, even though there's no real suspense and all motivation is as plain as a road map. There's no

THE LONGEST KISS ON TV, WITH JACK EIGEN. FEBRUARY 1954.

high-powered dramatic talent on display either, though the three principals manage well enough with roles that give them remarkably little to do. It is just the basic human situation itself that carries an ineradicable wallop. You may smile at the crudities of this film, but you're not likely to leave till you've seen the end of it."[47]

While she was in Chicago to publicize *Bait*, she was interviewed by Jack Eigen for his television show. The show was taped on February 16. At one moment during the interview the talk got around to movie censorship and the imposed limits on film kisses. Eigen then suggested that he and Cleo go for the record over live TV. This resulted in the famous 'five-minute' kiss. After the show hundreds of complaints came

47. *Brooklyn Eagle*, February 24, 1954.

in from viewers and the story made front pages around the country. Eigen refused to apologize for the kiss that some viewers described as coarse and vulgar, and he claimed that he had approval for the two minutes ahead of time from his wife of eighteen years. Eventually Eigen was fired from Chicago's Channel 7. In a telegram, the station said: "Due to the extreme poor taste, that under no circumstances can be considered

CLEO GIVES OUT KISSES TO THE CUSTOMERS OF THE HOLIDAY THEATRE IN NEW YORK CITY. FEBRUARY 1954.

acceptable TV fare in the homes of our viewers, we must terminate your services as of Monday."

Cleo successfully exploited the incident for months. "I got a letter from Jack's wife later saying he never kissed as good as that at home." Cleo even used the incident to underline her ambitions of becoming the governor of Louisiana. In an article called 'Atom Blonde Has Eye on Governor's Chair — Cleo Moore Threatens to Use Long Kiss as Campaign Weapon,' she was quoted as saying, "Personally, I don't see anything wrong in kissing. We teach babies how to kiss, and I knew how to kiss before I knew how to talk, and I would rather kiss than talk. If I always did, I'd never be in any arguments." Cleo predicted in the article that within five years' time, she would return to her birthplace to run for governor. She said, "I can't see how I can lose. All my relatives in Louisiana are in politics, and I'm related to 75 percent of the population. I spend my summers there and I'm campaigning already. If any woman tries to be governor before me, I'll campaign against her, even if I have to travel all over the state giving out my long kiss."[48]

In March 1954 Cleo was announced to star in Haas's newest production, *Hit and Run*. He decided to postpone this production and signed Cleo for another movie. "Hugo Haas put his *Hit and Run* story on the shelf in favor of a Hollywood yarn entitled *Turmoil*. It's about an ambitious young actress, and he's trying to sign Cleo Moore for the part."[49] *Turmoil* was released as *The Other Woman*. It was distributed by 20th Century-Fox and is considered a minor 'film noir'. It tells the story of a struggling starlet, who blackmails a director. The movie was filmed between April 1 and April 14. Cleo played the part of Sherry Stewart, a bitter, vindictive, intelligent psychopath very convincingly. Her movies with Haas consistently received fair to poor reviews, but they proved to be money makers. Once again, she was cast as a bad blonde. When she was asked about this typecasting, she answered, "They're better training than the gaga ingénues other girls are forced to play."[50]

By now Cleo's career was progressing nicely. She was named one of the most promising actresses for the New Year. Cleo began to believe that all her hard work was finally being rewarded. Producer Leonard Goldstein was scheduling his first movie with Cleo under her long-term contract. She was to star in a melodrama with Lee Marvin, called *Black Tuesday*. The script was ready to be filmed. It dealt with eleven o'clock on Tuesday nights, electrocution time, when the lights dim out and the scores of justice are settled. Goldstein was negotiating with Spyros Skouras to release the picture under the 20th Century-Fox banner. When negotiations with Skouras failed, Goldstein set up a meeting with Howard Hughes, the eccentric studio boss of RKO studios. Columnist Hedda Hopper announced on April 20 that the two men concluded a deal which called for ten pictures a year. Cleo was announced to star in one of the productions in the pact, *The Daughter of Diamond Lil*. Hedda mentioned that, "Cleo is blonde and beautiful and should fit neatly into the follow-up role originated by Mae West. Leonard tells me he is concocting this original himself and it's long

48. *Toledo Blade*, September 5, 1954.

49. *Times-Picayune*, March 5, 1954.

50. *Picturegoer*, November 27, 1954.

been a favorite project."[51] The movie with Lee Marvin was also mentioned to be released through RKO.

Next to her association with Leonard Goldstein, Cleo was still partnering with Hugo Haas. Hugo negotiated with Harry Cohn, and Cleo hoped to capitalize on that deal, too. She believed, and tried to convince herself, that she was on the verge of stardom. "I made a picture called *Bait* for Hugo Haas which Columbia was releasing and they sent me to New York to help plug it. My schedule was so tight I hardly had time to eat. I used to gulp sandwiches in taxis between appointments as I dashed from TV show to a guest spot on a disc jockey-show. When it was all over, though, the head of the publicity department was so appreciative of my cooperation and the way I handled myself, he urged the studio to put me under contract."[52]

Columbia Pictures formally announced on April 21, that Cleo was signed to an exclusive long-term contract. Immediately afterwards the statement was disputed by producer Leonard Goldstein, president of Panoramic Pictures, who contracted Cleo two months earlier. He stated, "There's a chance she'll go over there, but I haven't released her yet and will have to see Columbia's contract with her before I do so." After a meeting Goldstein annulled Cleo's contract. After negotiations with 20th Century-Fox and RKO, he formalized a deal with United Artists to produce ten films before he suddenly died from a cerebral haemorrhage on July 23, 1954. Goldstein was 51 years old. Cleo attended his funeral at the Church of the Recessional in Forest Lawn. Cleo and Ann Blyth were among the young ladies he had helped, and they stood outside the church, weeping bitterly over his sudden death.

LADY LUCK'S STEPCHILD

In Hollywood it was no secret that Harry Cohn was having problems with his number one money-maker, Rita Hayworth. Rita declined the parts that were offered to her, so Cohn confronted her that it was due to him that she had become a star. He made it even more clear that he could also break her. A similar situation had occurred at 20th Century-Fox a year earlier. There, Daryl Zanuck and Spyros Skouras had replaced Betty Grable with blonde starlet Marilyn Monroe. Cleo silently hoped that now was her time to reach stardom, too.

51. *Buffalo Courier-Express*, April 21, 1954.

52. *The Miami News*, March 7, 1955.

Columbia's studio head Harry Cohn had once let Marilyn go, for which he still blamed himself. He proclaimed that he could make any girl as big as Marilyn. Cleo hoped he would consider her and she was warming up to enter the 'Battle of the Blondes.' But Cohn was persuaded by his publicity men that Marilyn Pauline Novak was the girl to compete with Marilyn. As a result, Cleo lost a possible starring role in the noir crime film *Pushover* (1954) to the young newcomer. Jules Schermer remembered, "At the time I produced *Pushover* for Columbia, we knew it wasn't going to be a big picture because we only had a budget of $500,000 to do it. We were fortunate enough to get Fred MacMurray for the male lead and that took $60,000 right off the top for his salary. We needed a female lead. Obviously, we couldn't pay top dollar. We looked over the contract list and interviewed about ten girls for the role. Out of all of the girls, only one, Marilyn [Kim] Novak, pleased me. I guess I would have to say that she fell into the sex symbol category, as far as a description goes, because she oozed with sex appeal which we felt the role needed."[53]

Reviewing her debut in *Pushover*, *Variety* commented: "Miss Novak who reportedly is being groomed as a possible rival of Marilyn Monroe, shows possibilities in that direction." When the public also took a liking to Kim, she was rushed into other productions. Actor Steve Hayes recalled, "Kim Novak I met before she was put under contract at Columbia by mogul, Harry Cohn. She was sweet and rather shy. Our mutual contact was a film editor named Max who I'd known for years. She was catapulted to fame over several young starlets, like Cleo, I believe, due to her huge success in *Picnic*. She truly was stunningly beautiful, and not a bad actress eventually."[54]

Cleo sensed that her days as a threat to Marilyn Monroe were numbered. Instead of landing a starring role in a quality picture, Cleo was cast in *Women's Prison* with Ida Lupino and Jan Sterling. She was one of the inmates in the movie dealing with a crusading psychiatrist battling a sadistic female warden to improve conditions for the woman prisoners. Filming started in the Summer of 1954. One of Cleo's earlier movies, *One Girl's Confession*, had seen Cleo in prison also and the bad blonde tag that was put upon her hastened Cleo to remark, "In the forthcoming *Women's Prison,* I play a beautiful, young, innocent killer. But one day I would like to give up this type of role and play a nun."[55]

53. Kleno, Larry. *Kim Novak on Camera.* San Diego/New York; A.S. Barnes & Company, Inc., 1980.

54. Source: email contact with author.

55. *Toledo Blade*, September 5, 1954.

ARRIVING AT DEARBORN STATION
IN CHICAGO, PROMOTING *WOMEN'S PRISON*,
JANUARY 20, 1955.

Newspapers rumoured about the clash that was between Cleo and starlet Joyce Johnson. One article read, "Everybody will be watching with interest if Cleo Moore and Joyce Johnson have any scenes together in *Women's Prison*. Cleo is steady dating Travis Kleefeld now, but back in the days of her romance with Al Mathes, she was none too happy when Al started dating Joyce."[56] Joyce and Cleo had to disappoint the press, because the girls got along fine.

Travis Kleefeld was a wealthy building contractor Cleo had met through her father's builders' connections. He turned to singing and made his debut as Tony Travis on Dinah Shore's TV show. He was once engaged to actress Jane Wyman. Mr. Kleefeld reminisced, "I don't remember exactly how I met Cleo, but we were together for a while. I remember her with good thoughts. We were close for a while. I was a fan of hers, I thought she was lovely. I don't have a lot of memories, but we did have a romance and did date each other for a certain period of time. I thought she was a lovely person."[57] Mr. Kleefeld didn't recall why the romance ended. He remembered Cleo as a bright girl. She discussed her interest in politics with him and shared her feministic views on women having careers. She expressed how she tried to keep up on current events and told him she wasn't kidding about her hopes to someday run for office in her home state, Louisiana. She proclaimed that it's a woman's job to keep informed about the world and not just her own small circle of activities, whether it be the home, a movie set, or an office in which she works as a secretary. In an interview she unfolded her plans for 'The Pelican State.' "I have six more years to go on my movie contract, but after that I'm going to jump right into politics. First thing I'll do is close all the gravel and dirt roads in Louisiana and build the best four-lane superhighways in the country. A lot of my relatives live at the end of those dirt roads and it takes too much time to visit them."[58] She talked about the school problems and the 'right to work' bill. She said she had received messages from all over the country since her appearance on a TV show, where she had announced her intention to run for governor. "I've already got a lot of backers. If this keeps up, I may forget acting altogether and become a full-time politician."

The Columbia contract proved to be a trap. They did not intend to build up her career. Cleo was kept busy with personal appearances and posing for

56. August 13, 1954.

57. Source: telephone conversation with author, 10-08-2017.

58. *United Press*, March 5, 1955.

cheesecake photos. She was unhappy with this, and commented, "When you're a blonde and mother nature has been good to you, you have a chance in the movie business. But the biggest problem is that producers still think that blondes can't act. Since someone came up with the tag 'dumb blonde,' the whole of America seems convinced that the lot of us actresses are dumb broads."[59] Talking things over with Hugo Haas, he told her about

CLEO AND TONY TRAVIS, JANUARY 1955.

a script he was writing. She asked permission to do a movie outside the studio. Columbia agreed.

Because of the success of *Bait*, Hugo Haas signed John Agar to pair up with Cleo again. Hugo negotiated with Universal Studios to release his newest production. While filming *Hold Back Tomorrow*, in the winter of 1954, Cleo was allowed to attend the acting, dancing and singing classes at the studio. Mamie Van Doren and Kathleen Hughes were under contract to the studio at that time. Kathleen, who had worked with Cleo when they were making *Thy Neighbor's Wife*, met her on the studio lot. "I knew Cleo. She was taking some classes at Universal when I was there too. I saw her many times at the studio."[60] While study-

59. *Piccolo*, December 1955

60. Source: email contact with author.

ing at Universal studios, Cleo befriended Charles Simonelli. He was a producer who worked at Universal from 1945 until 1962. The two were seen dining out for the next couple of months. Their romance lasted a year. When Hugo Haas thought he would not be able to sell his picture, *Tender Hearts* — which was released as *Edge of Hell* — Cleo contacted Simonelli and asked him to see the film. A few days later, the studio

CLEO AND DJ JOHNNY KING, PROVIDENCE, RHODE ISLAND. APRIL, 1955.

bought it outright. *Edge of Hell* (1956) is one of the few Haas pictures in which Cleo didn't star.

In 1955, Cleo toured the country to promote Columbia's *Women's Prison*. On February 10, she visited Niagara Falls, where she autographed photographs in the Strand Movie Theatre lobby. On March 25, Cleo arrived in Houston by train at the Southern Pacific Station. A trio of bearded cowboys, called the Outlaw Riders, approached the train that carried Cleo. The outlaws captured Cleo and kidnapped her to their hideout, the Rice Hotel. A *Houston Chronicle* photographer was there to capture the publicity stunt. In Houston, the red-blooded Texans nearly tore her clothes off when a dozen boys, aged 16 or 17, wanted to be kissed by her and pulled a ruffle off her blouse as a souvenir. On April 7, Cleo visited Philadelphia and the tour ended on May 26, when she attended a screening of the movie in Providence, Rhode Island. By now, she was being called the 'Long

RECEIVING THE GOLD HERALD KEY
AS HONORARY EDITOR,
PROVIDENCE, RHODE ISLAND. APRIL 1955.

Kiss Girl,' due to the publicity stunt with Jack Eigen. While on tour she repeated the stunt with a newspaper reporter in New Orleans, with a kiss lasting six-and-a-half minutes. Subsequently, she kissed George Jessel, Bob Hope, Ezio Pinza and scores of reporters whom she probably would not have kissed otherwise. "My worst experience was after the opening of a picture here at the Holiday Theater when the ads said, 'Get a Kiss from

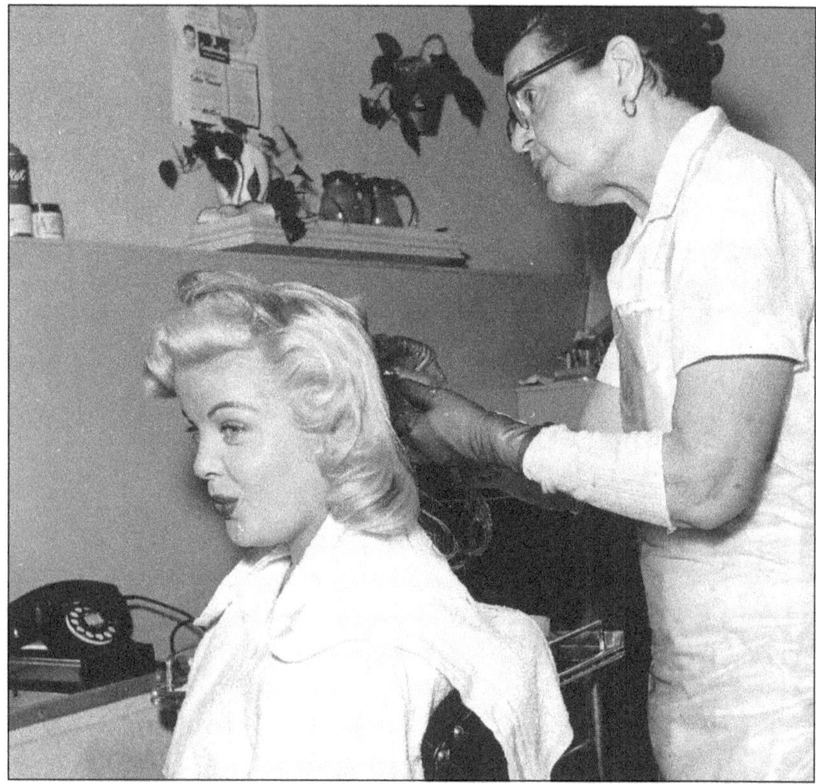

Cleo Moore in Person.' Actually, I was giving out candy kisses. One man grabbed me around the throat and said, 'I won't settle for that — I want the real thing.' We got rid of him."[61] Of related interest, Cleo noted this had become a problem when she traveled. "Ever since that Jack Eigen kiss incident, people don't ask me for my autograph anymore. They want a lip print for their autograph books. I'm a sport; I go along. So I end up using about ten tubes of lipstick a day. I've even had to buy a darker kind than I prefer to wear in order to make a better print." The tour was quite exhausting for Cleo; she had to visit a doctor in Miami because she was overtired.

61. *New York Post*, May 29, 1955.

CLEO GOES BRUNETTE, JULY 1955.

When Columbia Pictures sent Cleo on the road to exploit her pictures, she didn't mind. "But when they had me travelling all over selling Jimmy Stewart in *The Man from Laramie*, a picture I wasn't even in, and then wouldn't give me any good parts of my own, I rebelled," Cleo stated firmly. Because of Cleo's rebellion, Columbia re-considered if they had a suitable script laying around for her. They thought about starring her in a film biography on Jean Harlow's life. Marilyn Monroe had declined the offer

CLEO AND FRANCHOT TONE, JULY 1955.

to star at Fox and Columbia decided to put the project back on the shelf. In 1956, Kim Novak was considered. A year later, Jayne Mansfield and Barbara Nichols also showed interest to play the 1930s blonde bombshell who died at the age of 26. Cleo would have been perfect for the role. Just like Harlow's, her screen persona was that of a tough but sympathetic blonde. *The Jean Harlow Story* did finally see the light of day in the midsixties, when not one, but two movies were made, starring respectively Carroll Baker and Carol Lynley.

In June, Columbia announced that they picked up Cleo's option and planned to star her in *Siren Song*, an original screenplay by Richard Sale and Anita Loos. The latter also wrote *Gentlemen Prefer Blondes*. With *The Man from Laramie* set to premiere in San Antonio, Texas, James Stewart, co-star Donald Crisp and starlets, Kathy Grant, Lucy Marlow, Constance

Towers and Cleo, embarked on a tour of the state to promote the opening. Besides San Antonio, they also made stops in Houston, Dallas and Fort Worth. The three-day tour lasted between July 13 and 15. In Houston, a press breakfast, afternoon Western-style parade and the big night opening at the Majestic Theatre was the basis of the program. Between times, Stewart, Crisp, producer Bill Goetz and the Columbia actresses made television and radio appearances.

Siren Song was said to have been especially written for Cleo. Cleo jumped at this opportunity. She rehearsed her lines, took drama lessons, dieted, and worked out in the gym to lose weight. She worked on the movie between October 11 and October 24. When finished, the movie was re-titled *Over-Exposed*. Cleo played once model, now photographer Lila Crane who finds herself in trouble with the mob, because she has shot some compromising photos. Her gowns were especially designed for her by fashion designer Jean-Louis.[62] Cleo looked stunningly beautiful in the movie, and she hoped that this would be the breakthrough film for her. When she was asked if her career would obstruct possible marriage prospects, she answered, "You can't escape true love. You can decide to fight against it, but in the end you will lose. I just hope I won't fall in love, because there are so many things I still want to do. I still hope to become a big star. That has always been my biggest dream in life, to reach the top in my profession."[63]

Now that Cleo seemed to have reached the goal for which she had been aiming for, there was time for retrospection. She recalled her disappointments, frustrations, and her accomplishments. "Acting is hard work, with long hours. You must exercise and diet, and when these become a struggle, they affect you emotionally. Even when you are a top star, the battle never ends, because you know you can sustain your high position only so long as your work before the camera results in good box-office. Most important of all, acting requires great discipline, and often sacrifice, and you must be solidly equipped to bear through its sometimes seemingly unreasonable demands. Your moments of joy are often far outweighed by your hours of doubt and depression."[64]

62. French born fashion designer Jean Louis (1907-1997) designed the black strapless dress Rita Hayworth wore in *Gilda* (1946). He dressed Kim Novak in *The Eddie Duchin Story* (1956), *Jeanne Eagles* (1957) and *Pal Joey* (1957). He was famous for his beaded, nude dresses worn by Marlene Dietrich and Marilyn Monroe, when she sang "Happy Birthday Mr. President" to John F. Kennedy in 1962.

63. *Piccolo*, December 1955.

64. *Hollywood Stars*, 1955.

Hold Back Tomorrow had its world premiere at Detroit's Broadway Capitol Theater on November 3, 1955. To promote the movie, Cleo toured 66 cities with co-star John Agar. Several film critics gave Cleo and the movie a good review. "When I played a scene with apparently dark, because soaking wet, hair in *Hold Back Tomorrow*, critics really noticed me. They called me an actress of rare talent. It seems to me this is something that can't depend on the color of my hair?!"[65] Cleo was proud of her work in the movie. It allowed her to show her skills as an actress, dealing with a story about a convicted murderer and his last wish to spend one evening with a girl before he is hanged. It was a controversial subject and Cleo played the suicidal, knocked down by life character, convincingly. But the public wasn't convinced by the prison drama, and they stayed away.

Earl Wilson, mentioned in his syndicated column 'It Happened Last Night,' that, "Miss Cleo Moore, the Long-Kiss actress, is probably going to be elected 'Sing Sing Sweetheart' or 'The Prisoners' Pinup' since she started advocating that convicts be allowed to spend weekends with their wives or girlfriends. "I've already got a lot of fan mail from prisoners who want to talk the whole thing over with me and want to make an appointment," blonde Cleo told me during a visit to New York. Miss Moore insists that she's totally unselfish in this matter and that if she doesn't accomplish it now…"Just wait till I become Governor of Louisiana!" Pointing out that in Mexico, France, Switzerland, and several South American countries, the prisoners are permitted to see their mates for a day or two instead of just a half hour through a screen, Miss Moore says, "Here in the United States we don't pay the least bit of attention to a man's emotions." "Would you have husbands visiting women prisoners?" I asked Cleo. "Certainly! Women need somebody to love them more than men," said Cleo, bouncily. "Would you have women visiting husbands at Alcatraz where women aren't permitted now at all?" "No, the very bad prisoners should lose the privilege." Perhaps at this time I should let you in on a secret. Cleo's in a movie. *Hold Back Tomorrow*, in which she plays a gal who visits a prisoner in an unnamed country. In fact, she's been in several prison movies and feels like an ex-convict much of the time. "I can see the good sense of having special guest houses for prisoners when their wives come to see them," Cleo said. "Then when the prisoners come out they would be normal and able to lead normal lives again." Cleo claims that she became interested in this cause after Sheilah Graham's husband, whom Sheilah calls 'Bow-Wow,' and whom other people call 'Bow' for short, began advancing it. He is a social

65. *Piccolo*, December 1955.

welfare expert who argues that womanless, loveless prisoners are being punished beyond decency. "Don't forget that in some countries, men are even permitted to leave the prison for a few days for good behavior," Cleo mentioned. Cleo continues to insist that, as the ex-wife of Huey Long's son Palmer, she's going to run for Governor of Louisiana. "But I have to wait till I'm 30. I'm going to run and I'm going to win" she said. "I'll make

CLEO WITH MISS HOUSTON, SUE CAROL BROGIER AND STARLET KATHRYN GRANDSTAFF/GRANT, JULY 1955.

you a bet of a long kiss you'll never run," I said. "Why?" "Because when you're 30, you'll never admit it," I replied. "I'll admit it, but the question is," she said, "when I'm 30, will you still want to collect the bet?"[66]

To publicize *Over-Exposed*, Cleo attended the premiere of *Guys and Dolls* at the Paramount Theatre, on November 22. Working as a United Press photographer at the star-studded premiere Cleo stopped the show cold. She wore a strapless gold gown with a plunging neckline and clicked off twenty-four pictures of attending celebrities, before she joined her colleagues for the screening of the musical. On November 27, Cleo attended the annual *Modern Screen* awards evening. She witnessed Kim Novak winning the award for 'most promising newcomer.' Cleo had a strong feeling that her career in Hollywood was coming to an end. She had turned 32 recently, and she was surpassed by girls who were ten years younger. Her talking of leaving the movie business to go into politics didn't help to be picked for new assignments either. Unbeknownst to the fact, Cleo walked on a soundstage for the last time in December. Hugo Haas had rounded up the casting for *Hit and Run*, and filming commenced around December 10.

February 22 had marked the kick-off of her personal tour to promote *Over-Exposed*. Milwaukee was the first city she visited. The other day *The Milwaukee Journal* wrote about Cleo's sensational appearance. "By 4.55 p.m., when the train arrived, camera fans swarmed through the station and out on the tracks. There were at least 50, and perhaps 75, carrying a variety of cameras. The train pulled in and the photographers clustered around a rear car. Out came a hair dryer, ten pieces of luggage, a publicity man with a fur coat and then Miss Moore. Still playing the title role in her picture, the generously proportioned blond was wearing only a black chorus girl outfit and black net stockings. The temperature was 22. Cameras started to flash and click. Miss Moore ignored the cold and went thisaway and thataway, always wearing the professional model's smile. After a good fifteen minutes of this, Doug Taussig, the publicity man, protested, and held out a fur coat. "It's too cold," he said. Let's go inside the station." Miss Moore waved him off. "Gee, I love you!" yelled a boy. Miss Moore looked around. She had a pleased smile. Finally, Taussig prevailed. Wearing the coat, Miss Moore walked as far as the station shed, which was a few degrees warmer. She shed the coat again and the camera clicking resumed. The fans milled around her. She struck one pose, then another, pausing to sign autographs.

66. *Desert Sun*, November 26, 1955.

RIGHT: CLEO AT THE HOLLYWOOD OPENING OF *GUYS AND DOLLS*, DECEMBER 2, 1955.

PRESS
GUYS and DOLLS

After almost half an hour, Taussig finally had enough. He got the coat on Miss Moore again and she went through the station to a car." Cleo would visit eleven other cities in the United States. She ended her tour in Canada. The first city she visited was Ottawa, were she stayed for two days. Her Canadian trip included three other cities: Toronto, Hamilton and Montreal. In the last city she stayed four days and made several personal appearances.

Over-Exposed was released in April 1956. It was played as the second half of a double bill with Bill Haley's *Rock Around the Clock*. Columbia

DANCING WITH SAMMY DAVIS JR.

showed no further interest in Cleo's career. They had not handed her a new script or come up with a story written for her. Kim Novak got the star treatment at the studio, working with Tyrone Power in *The Eddie Duchin Story* (1956) and being announced for *Jeanne Eagles* (1957) with Jeff Chandler. At the time, Cleo told the press, "I'm tired of being treated like a dumb blonde. I want parts like Kim Novak gets. I'm sure I can handle them."

Bad publicity came in the form of a nasty publication. Scandal magazine *The Lowdown* picked up upon Cleo's statements about running for governor and especially about her idea of letting prisoners see their wives for some romance. They headlined their article, "With Bloody Prison Riots Raging Throughout the Country Cleo Moore's 'Sex For Prisoners' Baloney Is Not Only Cruel, But Dangerous." The magazine judged that, "Cleo Moore, a big-busted, big-mouthed hunk of female flesh has absolutely put the final stamp on the most outrageous nasty bit of press-agentry. What she has done, for the sake of a few headlines to spark a new picture, is to set the beds of more than 100,000 convicts, immured in State and Federal prisons, to groaning." The article suggests that Cleo's press agent mis-used her appearances in *Hold Back Tomorrow*, and to some extent in *Women's Prison*, to sell her statements as empathy when it is all too clear that it is nothing more than self-publicity. "You might think she had made a deep study of the problem; you might also think that she feels deeply and keenly for the cons. But there is another thinking coming. It may well be that some slimy press agent suggested the penological pitch that Cleo used to gain headlines across the country. But no matter whether it was her idea or another's, it's all very cruel." The writer of the article blames her for giving false hope and false warmth to men who are frozen fast behind bars. He keeps on lashing out at Cleo and ends the article with a serious threat. "As dawn after dawn comes up like thunder, and as the cons turns restlessly while waiting for the prison whistle to blow, Cleo and her promise will be uppermost in their minds and in their despair. And in this will lodge a hideous revenge." Ending the article in bold letters, "The Lowdown double dares you to offer to spend a real night with a condemned killer who is going to die at dawn. Let's see you offer it! Until then, remember the 100,000 cons who are thinking of you desperately."[67]

The article in *The Lowdown* hurt her feelings. She didn't understand how anyone would mis-judge her good intentions. She was very much aware that she had planted stuff in the media to publicize herself, but in

67. Article by Michael Scott Renick. 'Cleo Moore: The Convicts Bosom Pal.' *The Lowdown — the facts they dare not tell you*, March-April 1956.

CLEO AND JAYNE MANSFIELD
IN NEW YORK, MARCH 21, 1956.

doing so she always stayed close to her own beliefs and her feelings for other people, especially the less fortunate. She stood tall and said to herself she had to make an effort to refuel her career once again. Without a gimmick to sell, Cleo made sure she stayed in the public eye by attending as many parties and events that would gain publicity, as possible. On March 21, Cleo attended the 28th Annual Academy Awards Show in New York City. Although she knew instinctively that her film career was nearing its

LEFT: CLEO AND JOE KIRKWOOD, FEBRUARY 1956.
RIGHT: CLEO AND JOE DIMAGGIO, MARCH 1956.

end, she posed seemingly happy with ten-year younger, up-and-coming blonde starlet Jayne Mansfield in front of a huge cut-out of the Oscar statue. At the time, Jayne was a huge success on Broadway in the play *Will Success Spoil Rock Hunter?*

Two days later Cleo attended the 'Ball of the Year,' a benefit for the Boys Towns of Italy, with Joe DiMaggio, Marilyn Monroe's ex-husband. The 'Ball of the Year' was held at the Waldorf-Astoria Hotel in New York. DiMaggio crowned actress Shirley Jones as 'Queen of the Boys Towns of Italy' later that evening. Joe and Marilyn had broken up in 1955, Cleo commented at that time, "I strongly believe that Marilyn's life in the public eye, and her desire for publicity, her hip swaying and other tricks are the main reason why her marriage ended. You don't have to doubt for a minute that Marilyn was dead serious when she married Joe, but I question if she was prepared to behave like a married woman. Joe DiMaggio is a good-hearted, honest guy who doesn't want all that ballyhoo. He wanted a wife, not a model. But please understand that I know Marilyn as an honest, serious, and kind girl. She is calm and pleasant to be around. I am curious how she will solve her love problems. It is obvious she loves Joe and I wouldn't be

surprised if they would reconcile in the near future. I do hope she will go back to being her old self."[68]

No longer competing with Marilyn and seeing new blondes dominating the newspapers and fan magazines with their publicity stunts, Cleo decided it was time to take matters in her own hands. She would not sit around and wait for good offers to come her way any longer. In March

PUBLICITY PHOTO, APRIL 1956.

she had formed and investment company for television and picture productions, Myco — My Company — Investment Company, Inc. Through Myco she was planning to invest in motion pictures and TV productions as a forerunner to her entry into independent production in both. At the time Cleo was still under contract to Columbia Pictures. With three years of her pact remaining, Cleo secured the rights to do at least one outside feature film per year independently, either as a co-producer for investment purposes or as star and co-producer of her own film.

Cleo accompanied Colonel L.K. Carson of the Marine Corps to the premier of *Hold Back the Night* on July 29, 1956. Colonel Wesley L. Fox

68. *Piccolo*, December 1955. Cleo's words proved to be prophetic, because at the end of her life Marilyn was very much involved with Joe, and it is he who placed roses at her tomb until the day that he died.

CLEO AT IDLEWILD AIRPORT.

attended the premiere also. "In addition to showing the movie, Camp Pendleton's Commanding General invited Hollywood down for an Open House and an all-day Dog and Pony show. Among the movie stars were two young starlets who would have personal escorts and be given the red-carpet treatment. "I reported in khakis and carried my blues for the evening affair. Pendleton assigned a corporal to escort Cleo Moore, my starlet was Joi Lansing. We were a foursome for the entire day and evening. This was my first time with a celebrity or as part of a special group, and it was pure enjoyment."[69] Colonel Fox remembered, "Cleo was with her Marine escort and always with Joi and me, but Joi got all of my attention and time. I don't remember much about Cleo other than she was good looking, personable, and seemed to enjoy her time with her Marine."[70] Joi not only got the attention of her soldier, she also outshone Cleo when making headlines because of the daring low-cut dress she wore for the occasion.

In the meantime, the blonde she had met three months earlier at the Oscars had signed a lucrative contract deal at Marilyn's studio, 20th Century-Fox. Jayne Mansfield had been a sensation on Broadway and was now on her way to become a movie star in Hollywood. Cleo's studio, Columbia, jumped on the bandwagon, by releasing a movie Jayne had made before she went to New York, *The Burglar*. Cleo was surpassed by new faces, younger girls who stepped in to take over the throne of Marilyn Monroe. She asked for and obtained a release from her Columbia contract because she was upset at having to turn down several loan-outs due to the fact that the studio pressed her into conducting the exhausting personal appearance tour for *Over-Exposed*. While she was on tour, Columbia negotiated with Swedish bombshell Anita Ekberg and signed her to a long-term contract. Now the studio had Kim Novak to compete with Marilyn, and Anita as their answer to Jayne Mansfield. There was no room left for Cleo. The press took notice and declared that there was a personal feud between Cleo and Anita. Cleo added some fuel to the fire by saying that, "None of the European girls, including Anita Ekberg, has anything not found on American girls as well."

Cleo and her new press agent, United Artists exploitation representative Ward Bentley, cooked up some publicity and scheduled several personal appearances to keep her name in the spotlight. When she could not find work before the cameras, Cleo focussed on her work in real-estate. In

69. Col. Wesley L. Fox. *Marine Rifleman — Forty-Three Years in the Corps.* US: Potomac Books, Inc.,2002.

70. Source: email contact with author.

addition to her own $100,000 estate, she heads an investment corporation which holds property valued at $250,000 and she considered embarking on a million-dollar sports centre in the San Fernando Valley. Cleo negotiated with friend Joe Kirkwood as participators in his Valley sports centre project. She once again made public that she planned to return to her

CLEO WITH COLONEL L.K. CARSON AT THE MOCAMBO IN JULY 1956.

home state, aiming to become a politician. In an interview she said, "That's one of the reasons why I want to go back in 1958 and re-establish my residence. Then in 1959 and 1960 I plan to stump the state and campaign." What will her platform be? "I'm going to promise the people of Louisiana more of everything, more of the finer things in life. My campaign slogan is going to be 'More with Moore' or 'What Louisiana Needs Is a Blonde

PRESS PREVIEW FOR RKO'S *BUNDLE OF JOY*, DECEMBER 1956.

in Baton Rouge.'"[71] But apart from all other businesses she was involved in, acting and moviemaking stayed her number one passion.

On Thursday, December 16, Cleo attended the premiere of *Anastasia*, at the Roxy Theatre in New York. Marilyn Monroe was also attending the premiere that evening. Marilyn was hailed for her acting in the dramatic *Bus Stop* and had recently returned from England where she had filmed *The Prince and the Showgirl* with Laurence Olivier. Seeing Marilyn at the premiere and being confronted by all the attention she got, made Cleo feel self-conscious and sad about the prospects for her own career. There were

71. Parade, July 8, 1956.

CLEO IN NEW ORLEANS, APRIL 1958.

no offers for new productions. Nevertheless, she smiled broadly when the flash bulbs of the press guys flashed. Melissa Hood Duhe remembers that "Meeting her I always see her as being disappointed. That she didn't get a bigger role in a movie or that she didn't get one of the things she wanted to. I look at it now and think that she probably…you know she wasn't a big star. She was just always disappointed by that."[72]

At the end of the year, *Photoplay* magazine was sympathetic towards her when they included a small article entitled: 'Lady Luck's Stepchild.' It read, "Cleo Moore is a girl who's had more hard luck than most in her movie career. First, under contract to Columbia Pictures, she found herself cast in one prison role after another until she began to feel like a girl convict. Released by Columbia at her request, Cleo had several offers from independent producers. There was talk of casting her in *The Jean Harlow Story* and in the re-make of *Red-Headed Woman*, the Katherine Brush novel that helped make a star of Jean. But neither bright promise materialized, and Cleo is still holding out against any more B pictures that might consign her to movie oblivion. With talent and looks, plus the ability and willingness to work hard, Cleo's one of the many stories that happen in Hollywood which seem to have no explanation. Maybe 1957 will be her lucky year."[73]

ONE GIRL'S CONFESSION

The *Photoplay* article underlined the fact that talent and hard work did not guarantee success. Cleo's latest film was released to the public. It proved to be her last collaboration with Hugo Haas. In *Hit and Run* she played the cheating wife of garage owner Haas, who romances his employee, Vince Edwards. Together they plan to get rid of Haas. The film was distributed by United Artists. Columbia brought Cleo back on the big screen in 1957 too, when they decided to re-release the serial *Congo Bill*. After ten years of working as an actress in Hollywood, Cleo's acting career was over.

To secure her income she orientated on other businesses besides realty. In March she decided to make an investment in a petticoat factory. She stated, "They have 100 machines going and can't fill the orders." As challenging as these new functions were, she could not let go of her childhood dream of becoming a famous movie star. For *The Press Photographer's*

---

72. Source: telephone conversation with author, 03-17-2020.

73. *Photoplay*, December 1956.

Annual Edition of 1957, Cleo bought a page wide advertisement, featuring her in a satin night gown with matching sheer nylon dressing gown. Under the page-filling photograph was written: "Thanks Fellas: You're always in my dreams…Cleo Moore." It almost looked like she said goodbye to Hollywood with this advertisement, thanking the press for always staying loyal to her. Keeping herself in the public eye had always been a way for her to obtain contracts and movie offers. The advertisement was either a

CLEO IN NEW ORLEANS, APRIL 1958.

way to say goodbye to Hollywood or an attempt to prolong her stay in Tinseltown. On the cover of the annual was a girl who had followed the same path as Cleo to publicize herself. She was tagged as "one of 1956's most photographed personalities." Her name: Jayne Mansfield.

During the daytime Cleo operated her tasks as investor in the hosier factory and helped her father with the bookkeeping and planning for his construction business. In the evenings she stayed with her family or went out on the town with her friend, actor John Smith. Cleo's also seen around town with actor Joey Forman.

Early April 1957, Cleo's world collapsed when she found out that she was pregnant. She had missed her period and contacted her family doctor.

Although she had been cautious with the men she dated and slept with, the test results showed that she was pregnant. Cleo doubted who the father was. The scandal that would come about if the press got word of her situation was something she dreaded as much as telling her parents. She confided in her sister Yvonne. They concluded that, because of their religious upbringing, abortion wasn't an option. Wanting to keep the secret in the family, Cleo, Yvonne and her parents gathered and discussed what to do with this situation. At the family meeting it was decided that Cleo would step out of the public eye, that she would move in with her parents where she would give birth. Once the child was born, her parents would take care of the baby. Cleo's seventeen-year-old sister Jonnie Mae was to be named the unwed mother of the child.

Cleo's mother Una confided in her friend Regina what had happened. Regina's daughter Melissa vaguely remembers that there was something the adults didn't want her to know. "There seems to have been something macabre that happened, but it was kept secret from me. I would have been fourteen. If Cleo had a child, my mother would have desperately tried to keep that from me since she knew I adored Cleo. I had just begun to date and had recently gone through puberty."[74]

Cleo laid low. Once in a while she dated or went out, as long as she could hide the signs of her pregnancy. In October she is seen at the Beverly Hilton's chic L'Escoffier Room, having dinner with Juan Rodriguez. Rodriguez was the son of the former substitute-president of Mexico, Abelardo Rodriguez. When asked by columnist Harrison Carroll about the nature of her friendship with Juan, Cleo tells him, "Juan is a very wonderful man, so kind and considerate, but I have too many obligations to get married." Motherhood and being a career-woman were the obligations Cleo hinted at. However, Walter Winchell wrote several weeks later that, "she's telling pals she will become Mrs. Juan Rodriguez soon." Cleo hoped to tie the knot with Juan, so her child would have a father and she could pick up her life again. On the other hand, she would be forced to give up her dreams of being an actress, when she would decide to raise the baby herself. On December 15, 1957, a little girl was born. Cleo named her Debra Lee. Jonnie re-named her Debbie, letting everyone believe the baby was hers.

One of the first times Cleo's name reappeared in the papers, was on March 16, 1958. Jerry Lewis, celebrating his birthday, appeared in the role of auctioneer at the Art Show Auction being held for the Muscular

74. Source: telephone conversation with author.

Dystrophy Fund in Palm Springs. Proceeds from the auction went to the charity. The auction offered oil paintings, water colors, sculptures, by famous stars of stage, screen and television, including Vanessa Brown, Pat Morrison, Walt Disney, Harold Lloyd Jr., Mr. and Mrs. Jean Negulesco, Red Skelton, Noel Coward, among others. Cleo donated one of her paintings. Cleo's first public re-entry to showbiz was on April 26, when she visited New Orleans for the benefit showing of the movie *South Pacific*. Cleo arranged an interview with *The New Orleans States* newspaper. She told the reporter that she was looking for a script she can film in Louisiana, to be produced by her own company Myco. Furthermore, she declared she has been studying government and that she's still serious to take part in the 1960 governor election in Louisiana. "I'll run 15 times if I have to. If just my relatives vote for me, I've got it made." She continued, "I always wished I was a man because I always wanted to be governor. But now a woman can do anything a man can do. Don't you think? Besides, all women take care of a budget, they take care of their husbands and children. Why, by instinct a woman should know what to do."[75] Accompanying the article are pictures with a radiant Cleo, smiling broadly while browsing through the *New Orleans Yellow Pages*.

Among the few who knew about Debra, was Hugo Haas. He had promised to help Cleo with her career once the baby was born. In August, columnist Mike Connolly reports that Cleo and Hugo were planning to co-produce a telefilm called *Mystery Girl*. Connolly quotes Cleo saying, "Imagine ME, playing an undercover girl!"[76] Joe Kirkwood was another who knew her secret. He helped her by giving her a small part in one of his TV shows about golf. In August, Cleo and actress Marjorie Durant are hostesses at the opening of his Bowling Centre near the intersection of Whitsett Avenue and Ventura Boulevard in Van Nuys, California. That same month Walter Winchell reports that former lover Tony Travis is taking her swimming at Burbank's Pickwick Park. The plans for the Moore/Haas TV pilot never materialized and the romance with Tony Travis ended that same year.

During 1958 Cleo was a client of the Mishkin Agency. They also represented Fay Spain, Jeff Chandler, Chuck Connors and Lee Marvin. The agency could not find any work for Cleo. When the year was out, Cleo decided it was time to leave her movie star days behind her. She enrolled at UCLA for night courses in law and psychology, in October.

75. *New Orleans States*, April 27, 1958.

76. *Desert Sun*, August 22, 1958.

CLEO IN NEW ORLEANS,
APRIL 1958.

Cleo moved out of her parents' home, leaving one-year-old Debra Lee with her parents. On October 7, Cleo learned that her steady date Juan Rodriguez had been in a plane crash. He had survived the accident and was taken to hospital. Cleo rushed over to see him; she visited him regularly and helped him while he was recuperating of his injuries. In January 1959, Rodriguez is recovered well enough to take Cleo to Jack Denison's nightclub and restaurant. They arrive just in time to hear Denison's wife, Dorothy Dandridge, sing a telephone duet with Sammy Davis, Jr., who called from Las Vegas.

On June 18, 1959, Cleo attends the wedding of her sister Mary Lea and 26-year-old UCLA professor Bob Edgerton in Van Nuys. Jonnie Mae is a flower girl, Cleo was chaperoned by Yvonne's husband. Yvonne herself attended the wedding but didn't want to be included in photos for the media.

In September Harrison Carroll reports that Cleo is dating Anthony T. Carsola, a lawyer, and tells that it is the first time in many months that he saw Cleo with anybody but Juan Rodriguez. "Juan and I have decided not to date each other exclusively," Cleo commented. "Undoubtedly we'll be seeing each other from time to time. I think Juan is a wonderful fellow." With Juan recovering day by day, disaster strikes again when, on October 2, Cleo is involved in a traffic accident herself. Another driver ploughed into her car while she was waiting at the stop light, and she was thrown against the steering wheel. Causing her head, neck, back and chest injuries. Cleo was hospitalized for almost two months at St. John's Hospital. Doctors thought she had a bleeding ulcer, but that turned out to be internal bleedings. Juan Rodriguez calls her almost every day from Mexico, but he didn't visit her while she was in hospital.

Due to the automobile accident she has to cancel her trip to Manila to appear in the picture *This Side of Yesterday*. On February 8, 1960, Cleo files a $175,000 superior court suit over accident injuries she said hurt her career. Her complaint charged that Eugene Landis of the Mission Park Co. struck her car from the rear, causing her head, neck, back and chest injuries. She pleaded financial compensation because she was hospitalized and lost her income.

On May 19, Cleo is vacationing at the Americana Hotel in Bal Harbour, Miami Beach. She states that she "finds Florida more conducive to rest and relaxation than Hollywood." Cleo's Florida visit was not only for pleasure or leisure. She was out in Florida to meet Herbert Heftler. She had met him while making an industrial film, in Teaneck, New Jersey. Herbert was the President of Heftler Construction Company. He was intrigued by Cleo, who had impressed him with her experience and knowledge in building and selling houses. He found her to be pleasant company, and she was charmed when they discussed how he saw a future partnership in building and selling houses. Herbert had formed Heftler Homes and asked Cleo to partner with him in the company. He wanted her to become

a consultant, showing the houses to interested buyers. Apart from her consultant job, Herbert used her to advertise his projects. He advertised his homes with photos of Cleo in bikini and he gave potential buyers the chance to meet and greet the movie star Cleo Moore. Cleo held a big part in his campaigning for Heftler Homes in Florida. She was featured on the page-wide newspapers' advertisements.

True to her movie star persona, Cleo was at Brentwood Park where she welcomed the families interested in the houses on June 5. One week later she repeated her activities in Sunset Park. A newspaper announced that, "Miss Moore will give out autographed pictures to those requesting them, between 1 and 3 pm. At 3 pm the beautiful blonde will don a bathing suit and lead the parade to the Water Ski Thrill Show on Carol City's Lake." Back in Los Angeles in August she talks over her experiences with Herbert with good friend Al Mathes, while dining out at the Luau, Cleo's favorite restaurant in Beverly Hills.

Apart from working together, Cleo and Herbert began dating each other regularly over the next year. When she flies out East in September 1961, she is spotted by columnist Earl Wilson while lunching with Herbert at Blair House in New York City. They are profoundly serious about their relationship and discuss marriage, to be held on November 19. Herbert is nine years her senior. He is a widower with a 23-year-old son. The wedding took place at the home of the bridegroom's brother, George, an attorney, and was attended by friends and relatives. The civil ceremony was performed by Mayor Matthew Feldman. The couple announced that they were planning to live in Beverly Hills after their honeymoon in California.

Cleo wanted to raise Debra and picked her up at her parents' house. Four-year-old Debra came to live with her mother at the Coldwater Estate. Herbert knew of Cleo's secret. The couple decided to adopt Debra. Jonnie Mae, now twenty-one, had a hard time giving up 'her daughter.' Within the family the subject was never spoken of again. Cleo's nephew remembers about that time, "Sadly my family was very secretive, which I did not begin to realize until I was in college. There were many subjects that were never discussed, especially around the kids. I always thought that Debbie was Cleo's child. Whether I was told or assumed, I do not know."[77]

Sad news reaches Cleo when she learns that on June 10, 1964, Juan Rodriguez, 39 years old, was killed when his twin-engine plane hit a power line on take-off. The memory of Juan took her back to the time when

77. Source: email contact with author.

Debra was born. Although giving birth was the most special experience in her life, the remembrance was also mixed with feelings of sadness. Her film career ended brusquely, and she was forced to say goodbye to her life-long dream of becoming a famous movie star. Cleo would reminisce while browsing through her scrapbooks, thinking of her earlier life, and the way everything had changed. While doing so, she smoked several cigarettes and drank a glass of whiskey.

ACTRESS WEDS: Actress Cleo Moore, 32, and her new husband, builder Herbert Heftler, are planning to fly to California, weather permitting, for their honeymoon following their marriage yesterday by Mayor Matthew Feldman of Teaneck in that Township. Both had been married before. Miss Moore to Palmer Long, son of the late Senator Huey Long of Louisiana. Heftler, 46, was a widower. A reception was held at the home of Heftler's brother, George, at 1395 Sussex Road, Teaneck. (The Record photograph.)

NEWSPAPER ARTICLE WITH WEDDING PHOTO, NOVEMBER 20, 1961.

About six years into the marriage, problems occurred between Herbert and Cleo. Relatives and friends mention that the marriage was troubled. It was rumored Heftler had married Cleo for her name. He was said to have gained in his business by using her movie star image. Melissa Hood Duhe recalled, "Her marriage with Heftler was not happy. It seemed that he was using her. Her parents weren't very happy about it. He seemed to take advantage of Cleo and he wanted to use her as his own vehicle to go places."[78]

78. Source: telephone conversation with author, 03-17-2020.

Debra's school friend and neighbor Marie McCarthy mentions that she never met Herbert. "The portrait hanging in Cleo's den made him look like Robert Mitchum. I still don't know much about him. I wasn't allowed to visit when Mr. Heftler was home which was rare. He preferred to live in Florida and that broke Cleo's heart. She was a very lonely woman toward the end."[79]

Cleo's nephew, "In fact I was her favorite nephew. She told me that often," adds that the family didn't get together anymore that often since Cleo moved to Beverly Hills. "I did not see her too often, nor did we 'hang out.' Same, even more so with Mr. Heftler. Hardly ever saw him. He was nice but a tad aloof. We visited Cleo rarely once she married and moved to Beverly Hills. They seemed to live a life of luxury, with a large fancy house, maids and butlers, pristine furniture. Very nice. As best as I can remember though Mr Heftler was not around much, often away on business."[80]

Marie McCarthy remembers growing up with Debra in Beverly Hills. "My memories are around age nine or ten years old mostly. I went to live with my father when I was thirteen, but my mother was in Beverly Hills, and I would come back and forth. I was not around Cleo toward the end of her life." Marie remembers how Cleo loved to listen to Elvis Presley and that she loved watching TV. Old movies and lavish TV shows with show ballet, song and dance, were her favorites. "She also liked playing cards and taught us how to play Gin Rummy. I was fascinated by the way she shuffled cards like a pro. I remember when she would walk around the house or be sitting in her bed dressed in a non-see thru negligee or silk dressing gown. She had a very calm, glamorous way about her. I never heard her raise her voice once. She would only 'pout' when she was upset with 'Debra' as she sometimes called her. There was usually a burning cigarette or drink nearby in the afternoons. We all loved the pool, but she stayed out of the sun and could watch us swim on her bedroom TV through an outdoor camera. Usually, one of the maids would help keep watch. She stayed in her bedroom a lot. One of her favorite restaurants was 'The Luau' on Rodeo Dr., Beverly Hills, owned by Steve Crane. She threw Deb a birthday party there once."

"Debra and I were best friends and neighbors from kindergarten through 5th grade. We were still friends, but I changed school districts. I lived next door to Cleo Moore and Debbie. Cleo was a very glamorous woman even as a mother to Debbie. I loved her very much. Cleo was never a cutesy kind of woman. Also, very sexy, and smooth talking, even with

79. Source: email contact with author.

80. Source: email contact with author.

Deb. That was just her personality. I only saw her as a day-to-day Mom who really struggled. Debbie was somewhat out of control and pretty boy crazy at the time. Cleo had her hands full. Debbie was adopted by Cleo after she married Herbert Heftler. Supposedly Debbie was Cleo's sister's unwed child and Cleo raised her until the 'accident' or Cleo's death. Cleo gave Deb a different birthday. But the 'original' birth certificate said something different."

"Calling Deb 'boy crazy' isn't really nice. I should have said that we all were about that age when we were noticing the boys. Especially coming from a family where the father is not around much. When I would visit Debbie, she always wanted to go to Coldwater Park in Beverly Hills, just down the way from the house. Lily, the maid, had to go with us but that didn't keep us from sneaking away to the soda fountain shop at the Beverly Hills Hotel for a milkshake! Cleo never came down to the park except one time when she came looking for us in her car and we had been hanging out with the local kids up the street in Franklyn Canyon. Cleo wasn't pleased about that!"[81]

Although she was unhappy in the marriage, Cleo decided to stay for the sake of her daughter. Melissa Hood Duhe's mother had stayed in contact with Cleo, and they would speak to each other on the phone. "I think she would occasionally talk to her which usually provoked crying. My mother loved her so much. She hated that Cleo was unhappy. My mother felt responsible for Cleo going to Hollywood which was a double-edged sword."[82]

Cleo would return home to Louisiana sporadically over the years. Second Cousin Wendy Ortego remembers, "In the 1970s she didn't come back much. When Cleo did come home, momma said she came in a black limousine and practically begged my momma to go out with her."[83] Herbert Heftler never accompanied his wife when she would visit Louisiana.

When her mother suddenly died on February 28, 1973, Cleo sank into a depression. One morning Debra entered Cleo's bedroom, she found her mother not responding to her. On October 25, 1973, eight months after her mother's passing, Cleo Moore died from a heart attack, just 49 years old. When poor Debra found her mother, she ran to the telephone in panic and called her aunts. According to Debra, Mary Lea and Jonnie Mae arrived before the police did.

81. Source: email contact with author.

82. Source: email contact with author.

83. Source: email contact with author.

Marie McCarthy recalls that Debra had her own view of her mother's death. "Debra believes that her mother was murdered or was made to feel so miserable that she died. It's a possibility because one evening as we were in Cleo's private den off her bedroom, she had a — pink handled — revolver. I sensed she feared for her life."[84] In retrospect, the cause of, and circumstances around Cleo's death are pure speculation. At the time, most of the newspaper obituaries mentioned that the cause of death was not disclosed. *The Gonzales Weekly*, from Friday, November 16 mentioned that Cleo had died from a coronary arrest.

The loss of their mother and sister and Murphy's beloved wife and eldest daughter was a huge blow to the family. Una had been the strong force in her family. Cleo was the sister they had always looked up to. Now the three remaining sisters had to make out amongst themselves what to do with Debra. She could not stay with her stepfather Herbert. He put his mind to his work to cope with the loss of his wife, a wife he had neglected for the last years of their marriage. He didn't know what to do with 15-year-old Debra. Marie McCarthy recalls about that period, "Cleo's sister — we called her Tia — took Debbie to live with her and oversaw Debbie's money since she was a minor. I believe Deb was about fifteen years old. I didn't see much of Deb after she went to live with Tia. I went to live with my father and left LA at that time. But I think Debbie wanted to go live with her aunt. She wanted more freedom. Cleo was pretty housebound. Tia, I think her real name was Jonnie, wanted Deb to be her child and even renamed her Sonja when she went to live with her."[85]

Rumors within the family made Cleo's nephew believe that maybe Debra wasn't his Aunt Cleo's daughter after all. "Growing up, Debbie was presented as Cleo's daughter. As I got older though there were 'quiet' family whispers that Debbie was actually Jonnie Mae's daughter. After Cleo passed this intensified, again in family whispers. I was never directly or officially told."[86] Cleo's nephew believes that it was a family plot to protect underage Jonnie Mae and the entire family from the shame that would have followed in that day and culture. According to him, Cleo played her part and took her responsibility as the oldest sister.

Cleo's poodle Gigi and long-time maid Maria moved in with Yvonne and her family. Maria quickly became a beloved family member and stayed

---

84. Source: email contact with author.

85. Source: email contact with author.

86. Source: email contact with author.

with the Saunders for approximately six years, until a family emergency in Guatemala called her home.

Two years after Cleo had died, her belongings were offered for sale. In April 1975, there was an advertisement in the *Los Angeles Times* announcing the estate jewelry sale. Cleo's jewelry was sold to the public. Earrings, bracelets, necklaces, brooches and a Rolex watch were offered for a total price of $10,055. It is unknown who sold the jewelry to the '14 karat shop' seller.

UNA AND MURPHY MOORE.

Cleo's father, Murphy Charles Moore, died in 1978. That same year Heftler married his secretary, 33-year-old Monica Anderson. Monica resembled Cleo in facial features. In an interview Monica talks about how much she loved Herbert and his sense of humor. Herbert Heftler passed away on January 18, 1999, at the age of 85. Instead of the traditional funeral, Monica threw a gala party to celebrate his life. This lavish act drew criticism from some, but according to Monica, anyone who truly knew Herbert would have agreed that the affair was exactly what he would have wanted. In fact, Monica and Herbert were known for holding some outrageous parties.[87]

In the last ten years Debra spoke out about how her aunts Mary Lea and Jonnie Mae took all of her mother's estate before it went into probate. On the internet and her Facebook account, she mentions that Cleo was a loving mother and Herbert, "…was the best father in the world." Debra seems convinced that her mother was murdered. It looks like Debra is living a hard life. I contacted her a few times and communicated with her by email. She was friendly and promised to talk with me. This never happened unfortunately. It is she and Jonnie Mae who know about Cleo's life and what happened after her death. Cleo's sisters chose to stay silent about Debra's ancestry; I guess she will never know if Cleo was her mother or aunt. Now only heaven knows.

Yvonne died in 2008 and Marilea passed away three years later. Jonnie Mae passed away in August 2021, shortly after I tried to get in contact with her.

87. *www.socialmiami.com*

PUBLICITY PHOTO FOR STRANGE
FASCINATION, WITH HUGO HAAS.

Filmography

HUGO HAAS

Cleo Moore's name probably would not have been remembered today if it wasn't for Hugo Haas. The writer, producer, actor, and director cast her as his leading lady in seven of his films. His specialty was human interest stories, many of which had the central theme of an older man helping a younger girl, with usually tragic results. Haas used Cleo's sex appeal to advertise his movies, to give his dramatic stories some extra spice. According to Haas, "Cleo also possesses that magical, combustible something which made the wanton sirens of past days set the torch to the film fan's imagination. Today, the style has changed except for the electric sparks that lie underneath. Sex appeal is more direct. The plunging neckline, the sweater, slashed skirts and swimsuits have come into vogue. They're just as effective too."[1]

With every movie that Hugo made with Cleo, he provoked the Legion of Decency's guidelines. Cleo explained, "I'll leave playing simpering ingénues to anyone who wants 'em. Personally, I'd prefer a niche in the cinematic 'Hall of Flame,' along with Jean Harlow, Jane Russell, Mae West and Dagmar."[2]

Most of the Haas/Moore movies were highly suggestive in the scenes that dealt with sexuality. *Thy Neighbor's Wife* and *Strange Fascination* have no obvious sexy scenes, still the sexual refusal and tension between the older judge/pianist and the young bride/dancer is shown effectively in both movies. *One Girl's Confession* showed Cleo in her slip while undressing or relaxing in her room. Mary Adams was a character who pulled the strings

1 *Strange Fascination* pressbook.

2. *One Girl's Confession* pressbook.

when it came to romance and men's admiration. *Bait*'s Peggy was more vulnerable, depending on the protection of a man. Cleo's bathing scene in *Bait* caused a stir as it was a daring scene by fifties standards. Sherry, *The Other Woman*, is a conniving blonde starlet, a revengeful girl. Cleo is not featured in a bathing suit or lingerie throughout the picture; she really gets a chance to show her acting skills. The seduction and drugging scene

HUGO HAAS.

has some erotic overtones but is emphasizing the cunning nature of Cleo's character. The same goes for *Hold Back Tomorrow*. Cleo wears a torn dress and an overcoat; the focus isn't on Cleo's physique but on the dramatic storyline. Nothing highlights the sexual tension, but every scene with Cleo and John Agar hints towards the longing for tenderness and belonging to someone romantically. Her last outing with Haas, *Hit and Run*, is the

CLEO AND HUGO HAAS, 1953.

tamest version of a bad blonde. Her sexiest scene is at the beginning of the movie, where she is dressed in a showgirl outfit. The rest of the movie shows Cleo in plain house dresses. In several scenes the sexual tension between Vince Edwards and Cleo is shown, but this time Cleo tries to fight against it instead of provoking it herself.

The Haas films are trademarked by their triangle themes. His films possess a certain quality that puts them in the exceptional category. One is the simplicity of the story, with no flashbacks or techniques to amaze or possibly confuse the audience. Second, they are films designed for intelligent adults; third, the acting for the most part is spontaneous and natural; fourth, they were completed on lower budgets than some producers deem essential for short subjects.[3] Haas once commented, "Other

3. *International Photographer*, March 1952.

people specialize in musicals, or in westerns. I like to specialize in triangle stories, because they feature the vagaries of human nature and the ironies of circumstance."[4]

Haas produced, directed, wrote, and acted in most of his films. "I can make my pictures on a small budget because I don't have to pay four important salaries: producer, director, writer, banker. I take care of those departments and also throw in some acting. It saves as much as $125,000."[5] Jan Lowell remembered, "Hugo always rehearsed at home, so when we got into the

studio, we knew what we were doing. Short schedules, he often cut shorter. A hundred days, more or less."[6] His films were usually shot in ten days.

Hugo Haas was born on February 18, 1901, in Czechoslovakia. His father, who owned shoe stores in Brno, was Czech and his mother was Russian. Both parents loved the arts and educated Hugo and his brother Pavel along those lines. The Haas home was open to actors, writers, composers and singers before whom Hugo and Pavel gave piano concerts.

4. *LA Daily News*, September 15, 1953.

5. *The Cincinnati Enquirer*, March 25, 1956.

6. Source: email contact with author.

After finishing high school, he entered the State Conservatory of Music and Drama in Brno and the following year he received a contract from the Brno Municpal Theatre. He was a talented and respected actor and director in the 1930's, writing, directing and acting in approximately thirty films. In 1937 Haas married Maria Bibikoff, the daughter of the last Czarist ambassador to Berne, Switzerland. She was 19, he was 36.

Haas fled to the United States when the Nazis invaded his country. Leaving his brother Pavel, a prominent composer and pianist, and father

behind. Both men were killed in the gas chambers of Auschwitz. When he fled Prague in 1939 with his actress wife Bibi, they were forced to leave their three-week-old son Ivan, because the underground would not move children. Ivan was kept by a thirteen-year-old sister of Hugo's, until they were allowed to enter the United States, in October 1946.

During the war years Haas worked as an announcer on US broadcasts to the Eastern European underground. In 1943 he picked up his acting career, playing foreign villains in supporting roles. With the money he earned, he financed his own written, produced and directed films, for he believed that there was a sizeable neglected American audience in those who liked the European touch with film making but were annoyed at having to put up with subtitles. Therefore he decided to use his knowledge of the European technique, translated in the English language. He worked with a group of Eastern European film makers, many of whom fled the Nazis when they invaded their countries. Among his crew there were many who sympathized with Communism and Socialistic ideas. Haas didn't want to be blacklisted like the Hollywood Ten but employed his friends anyway. Jan Lowell recalled, "Hugo and Cleo were not touched by McCarthy. Of course, what was going on in Hollywood worried him, because he knew what had happened in Europe pre-WW2 and he was always fearful. As for Bob and me, we were not important enough to be blacklisted, but were what was called 'grey listed.' All our friends included the Hollywood Ten and even more and we were not quiet about how we felt. This made Hugo very nervous, but he still used us in his films. We just never talked politics."[7]

Czech film historian/journalist Pavel Taussig perceptively analyzed Haas's films. "Most of the characters he played later on were old men who were all alone and who nobody was interested in. These characters usually fell for a younger woman, but their love would invariably turn out to be nothing but a false illusion and they quickly ended up having to face the harsh reality of their situation. These scenarios pretty much tied in with Haas's own personal feelings about living abroad and the melancholy of his exile."[8]

Friend Jan Lowell loved Haas dearly. "Hugo was a warm, loving person, who enjoyed jokes and fun and laughing and loved life, but deep down inside him was always the tragic life left behind and his parents' and brother's death. I adored the man. He took my father's place and gave me away at my wedding."[9]

Actor/screenwriter Steve Hayes met Hugo Haas when he attended the coffee shop Googies, looking for new talent for his movies. "Hugo was very pleasant, with a slight accent. A big man, sadly overweight (like many folks in those days), but always a gentleman."[10] Haas greatly enjoyed working with young people and felt he had been fortunate most of the time in his selections of unknown actors. Haas commented on his practice to hire new names, "When a picture is made with an eye to costs, you can't afford big name stars. And if you make them with unknown, but talented newcomers,

7. Source: email contact with author.

8. Taussig, Pavel. *Hugo Haas: Život jako film.* Plus; 2015.

9. Source: email contact with author.

10. Source: email contact with author.

BAIT

for

Business!

CLEO MOORE AND RICK VALLIN
ON THE SET OF STRANGE FASCINATION.

no one will go to see them, unless tremendous sums are spent for exploitation. The logical solution is to introduce youngsters in co-starring roles with established stars." Lance Fuller and Vince Edwards are two of Cleo's co-stars who carved out a nice acting career for themselves, after appearing in a movie by Haas.

Actress Kathy Marlowe underlines Haas's kindness in helping young actors. She was picked out by Haas to play a small part in *Hit and Run.* Blonde Kathy was a struggling starlet when she met Haas in August 1955. "I was with Hugo, not romantic, it was more like a friendship, but I was with him a lot of nights, having acting lessons and I would talk to him about my various interviews. Everybody liked Hugo, because he gave all kind of people, who couldn't get a first part to get a Screen Actors Guild, he gave everybody a part even if it was small. He was really sympathetic to young actors."[11]

Besides giving new talent a chance, Haas also helped actors whose career had slowed down. Of course, it was also name value that helped to sell his movie. John Agar, for example, was down and out on his luck due to alcohol abuse when Hugo gave him a chance to appear in two of his movies.

Apart from giving actors a chance to play in his movies, Haas also attended acting classes to give out advice. Sometimes Cleo accompanied him. Actor/dancer Christopher Riordan remembers meeting them both at an acting class he attended, "Margot, a friend of mine asked me to come to acting class that she was taking in Cosmo Alley. That's a little street behind the Ivar Theatre in Hollywood. You had to enter from the back and climb an enormous amount of stairs. Margot was right. It was a fun class, and I began attending quite regularly. I recall, the teacher's name was Julie Gibson. She was a cute little lady, with a lot of energy. And, we had a lot of very talented people in those classes. I kept coming when time allowed. And on one of those evenings that I showed up, Julie had a couple of other guests that had appeared to speak to us, give us advice, and in general, support us all in our wishes to succeed. This time, she announced the week before, that visiting us 'next week' would be the actor/director, Hugo Haas, and his frequent leading lady, Cleo Moore. I wasn't sure what to expect. For one thing, I felt that Mr. Haas only did very small budget pictures. And, Ms. Moore was, in my opinion, another in the long line of blonde ladies that hoped to cash in on the popularity of Marilyn Monroe. All week, Margot kept asking me if I was going to come to the class. I

11. Source: telephone conversation with author, 9-22-2018.

didn't really think I would; but then Margot's car broke down, and she needed a ride. So, I went. And, I must say, I'm very glad I did. Mr. Haas was most informative. He really knew the ins and outs of the business. Acting, directing, producing, marketing, etc. He was a very intelligent guy. And Ms. Moore was nothing like what I had expected. After listening to her for a while, her blonde hair disappeared, and she sounded like any

CLEO IS TOUCHED UP BY MAKE-UP MAN TED COODLEY, ON THE SET OF *HIT AND RUN*, 1955.

other very intelligent businesswoman. She was not a sex symbol standing before us. Of course, she had more information to impart to the females in the class; but I took her words and kept them in my little head for many years. After the class, the two stayed on and listened to what we students had to say. They were both very patient, and very exacting in what knowledge they gave us. When the evening was over, I had a lot of respect for what Mr. Haas had accomplished in film making. And…a tremendous amount of admiration for what Ms. Moore had endured, accomplished, and given to all of us. She was a class act, to be sure. Nothing like the roles she couldn't escape."[12]

12. Source: email contact with author.

After Haas and Cleo had parted, he went to MGM to direct *Lizzie* (1957) and *Night of the Quarter Moon* (1959), with Eleanor Parker and Julie London respectively. When given more budget and time to make a film, and allowed to work with more experienced actors, Haas showed his unusual talent that was never fully recognized by Hollywood. Milan Hain commented, "They remain the only pictures Haas made outside his own company. Even though he had earlier claimed no interest in making films for other producers, the development in the American film industry of the 1950s convinced him otherwise. It became more and more difficult for Haas to obtain financing and secure distribution for his independent efforts."[13]

In the early sixties, Hugo Haas returned to Europe with his ex-wife Maria Bibikoff, taking up residence in Rome, Trieste and Vienna. There he made several TV films. In 1963 he returned to Czechoslovakia, but was saddened what he found there — politically, religiously, and theatrically.[14] He died in Prague in December 1968, several months after the Russian invasion of his homeland. His ashes are buried at the Jewish Cemetery in Brno.

"PICK-UP" – BEVERLY MICHAELS

Cleo's predecessor, 5-foot 9-inch Beverly Michaels was born in New York City on December 29 in 1928, the third of six children. She had two older brothers and three younger sisters. Her father was a bus conductor. She graduated from parochial grammar and high schools, was a good student and she'd wanted to attend college, but family finances were too limited. For her sixteenth birthday, her cousin took her to her first night club. It was Billy Rose's Diamond Horseshoe where the tall girls were billed as 'long stemmed American Beauties.' Beverly, about to graduate from high school, decided that show business was to be her business. She talked to the nightclub's manager and got a job as a hatcheck girl. Within a week she was out of the derby department and into the show line.

While working at the Horseshoe, she also started her modelling career. She became a Conover girl and because of her tall, handsome figure and small, photogenic features was soon in demand for high fashion

13. Milan Hain. *Hugo Haas — Forgotten Émigré.* Noir City, winter 2012.

14. Loutzenhiser, James K., *Hugo Haas — Sincere Artist Who Became Lost in the Hollywood Shuffle.* Article in *Films in Review*, February 1978.

photography. Additionally, she started studying dramatics and tap dancing. She landed herself a job as both showgirl and dancer with a troupe that went to Cuba, staying for ten months. In 1944 she had worked in a musical comedy stage show, with Eddie Foy Jr. and Jane Withers, called *Glad to See You*. When the show closed after eight weeks, she went back to night club shows, worked in Miami and Washington. When a friend

from the Horseshoe, Kay Crespi, was going to Hollywood for a screen test, Beverly went along. Her goal was legitimate theatre, but when it seemed she'd never make it, she didn't let her five-feet-nine discourage her from tackling motion pictures. She read for a featured role in *East Side, West Side* at MGM and got it. "My height helped me get it. As it turned out, they wanted a girl big enough to murder Ava Gardner. And I was."[15]

Beverly's career didn't really get started until *Pick-Up*. Haas had her wear her 'obvious' clothes for the picture at home for several days before production began. To get even more feeling for the character of the pick-up girl, he took her to bars down on Los Angeles' Skid Row to see the 'real thing.'

15. Photoplay, December 1952.

Pick-Up tells the story of lonely railroad manager Jan Horak, played by Haas, who falls for a floozie who is only interested in his life savings. She falls in love with a younger man, Allan Nixon, and sets out to ruin Horak. On September 12, 1950, Haas signed a releasing deal with Harry Cohn of Columbia studios. 20th Century-Fox also tried to get the rights to release the movie, but Joseph M. Schenk lost out to Cohn. The picture

ON THE SET OF *PICKUP*, 1950.

was made for approximately $85,000. Cohn bought it for $125,000. He made a million-dollar profit.

Beverly Michaels is unforgettably nasty and as hard-boiled as a 15-minute egg. She also improvised much of her own dialogue. Haas admitted in an interview that he simply asked the actress "to use language she thought appropriate to the situation." He took Allan Nixon and Beverly on several picnics to the Mojave Desert to rehearse. Many times, they would stop in the middle of a scene, changing the lines that were in the script. "I'd rephrase the lines until they sounded right for me and for the character I was playing. When Hugo said they sounded right to him, we'd shoot it," Beverly commented.[16] Hugo's wife Bibi studied

16. Daily News, July 9, 1950.

and rehearsed with Beverly at her home. The movie was shot in ten days, including the interior scenes at Motion Pictures center in March 1950.

The reviews for *Pick-Up* were favorable. "An unusually well-done shocker with strong impact" (*Screenland*). "The characterizations are well-defined and the acting by Haas, Miss Michaels and Nixon is highly competent" (*Motion Picture Daily*). *Pick-Up* earned a nomination from

the Writer's Guild of America for 'Best Low-Budget Screenplay." It lost to Samuel Fuller's *The Steel Helmet*.

Haas cast Beverly again in his next production, *Girl on the Bridge*. 20th Century-Fox promptly purchased the movie. Beverly played Clara, an unwed mother. She meets and marries Haas, a widower whose family was killed by the Nazis. The movie was released in November 1951. Beverly was enthusiastic about working with Haas. She remarked: "What a great director he is, I've been spoiled! We later made a second picture, but it was released by another company and didn't get much exploitation or attention. I played quite a different character in that, but people don't seem to know much about it."[17]

17. Screenland Plus TV-Land, December 1952.

After she had soared to success in *Pick-Up*, Beverly turned down two term contracts with major studios, mainly because they didn't give her the right to do an outside picture a year with Haas. Eventually Columbia took over her contract and let her sit it out. In September 1952 she asked for her release and signed a long-term contract with Universal-International. She was rumoured to be starred in a production called *Night Flower*, but it was never made. Mamie Van Doren, "Beverly was under contract to Universal when I entered the picture in January 1953. She was hard boiled, no acting required. I liked her then and still do. She was very striking looking in person. I remember her dark brown eyes."[18] After sitting around and doing nothing for months, Beverly asked for, and got, her release from Universal.

In 1952, Beverly had met writer and producer Russell Rouse, her future husband. Her part in *Pick-Up* proved to be good training when she was awarded with the leading part in Rouse's *Wicked Woman* (1953). Beverly played a sultry waitress in the film that was heavily influenced by her work with Haas and featured a memorable turn by Percy Helton in the role normally reserved for Haas. When interviewed on the set of *Wicked Woman*, Beverly told a newspaper reporter, "This is my first screen role since I asked for my release from a major studio contract and began to freelance. They gave me so little to do at the studio that this can be called my first movie role, actually. When I finish this, I am going to wait for another part like it, a bad girl role. Such a part gives an actress a chance to do things in a dramatic way. I won't take just anything that is offered. I'd rather do one good picture a year than half a dozen mediocre ones."[19]

Beverly Michaels appeared in a couple of B-movies and TV shows, before she decided to quit show business in 1956. She gave birth to two sons and a daughter. She became Rouse's widow in 1987. Twenty years later she died from a stroke.

18. Source: email contact with author.

19. Hollywood Citizen News, September 17, 1953.

THE FILMS

EMBRACEABLE YOU

1948 — Warner Bros.
80 minutes — Black and White

DIRECTOR: Felix Jacoves. PRODUCER: Saul Elkins. SCREENPLAY: Edna Anhalt, based on the story by Dietrich V. Hannekin and Aleck Block. PHOTOGRAPHY: Carl Guthrie. MUSIC: William Lava. EDITING: Thomas Reilly. ART DIRECTION: Ted Smith. SET DIRECTION: William Wallace. MAKEUP: Perc Westmore. SOUND: Stanley Jones. SCRIPT SUPERVISOR: Fred Applegate.

CAST: Dane Clark *(Eddie Novoc)*; Geraldine Brooks *(Marie Willens)*; S.Z. Sakall *(Sammy)*; Wallace Ford *(Police lieutenant Ferria)*; Richard Rober *(Sig Ketch)*; Lina Romay *(Libby Dennis)*; Douglas Kennedy *(Dr. Wirth)*; Mary Stuart *(Nurse Purdy)*; Philip Van Zandt *(Theatrical Agent Matt Hethron)*; Rod Rogers *(Bernie Sallin)*; Charles Williams *(Albert Martin)*; Charles McAvoy *(Bartender)*; **Cleo Moore** *(Sylvia)*; Janet Barrett *(Secretary)*; Dave Barry *(The Comic)*; Cliff Clark *(Honest Peterson)*.

STORY: A killer and his driver Eddie Novoc accidentally run over Marie Willens, while fleeing a murder scene. The pursuing detective Matt Hethron is sure that Eddie is guilty, but he cannot prove it. Instead of pressing his case, Hethron has Eddie begin caring for Marie who received a massive blood clot from the accident and does not have long to live. As time passes,

Eddie finds himself falling in love with Marie. To raise the needed money for her care, Eddie starts blackmailing gang kingpin Sig Ketch.

REVIEWS: There is considerable hokum in this rather routine romantic melodrama, which does not rise above the level of program fare, but its mixture of romance and gangster activities should satisfy generally as a supporting feature. The chief trouble with the story is that it lacks conviction because its development depends too heavily on coincidence. It manages, nevertheless, to hold one's interest fairly well, for one is sympathetic to the hero and heroine because of the hopelessness of their love, brought about by the heroine's impending death. *(Harrison's Reports)*

The story, obviously, is pretty preposterous. However, it manages to generate a lot of excitement, and furthermore it's quite a tearjerker. That will appeal to the ladies, and for the guys, there's Geraldine Brooks, who is really worth seeing." *(Modern Screen)*

NOTES: Released in July 1948. Working title *This Side of the Law*. In its April 3 issue, *Boxoffice* magazine mentions that Dick Bartell and Cleo Moore joined the cast.

CONGO BILL

1948 — Columbia
270 minutes — Black and White

DIRECTOR: Spencer Bennett and Thomas Carr. PRODUCER: Sam Katzman. SCREENPLAY: George H. Plympton, Arthur Hoerl and Lewis Clay, based upon the comic strip *Congo Bill*, appearing in the magazine *Action Comics*, created by Whitney Ellsworth. PHOTOGRAPHY: Ira H. Morgan. MUSIC: Misha Bakaleinikoff. EDITING: Earl Turner, Dwight Caldwell. SET DIRECTOR: Sidney Clifford.

CAST: Don McGuire *(Congo Bill)*; **Cleo Moore** *(Lureen aka Ruth Culver)*; Jack Ingram *(Cameron)*; I. Stanford Jolley *(Bernie McGraw)*; Leonard Penn *(Andre Bocar)*; Nelson Leigh *(Dr. Greenway)*; Charles King *(Kleeg)*; Armida *(Zaleea)*; Hugh Prosser *(Morelli)*; Neyle Morrow *(Kahla)*; Fred Graham *(Villabo)*; Rusty Wescoatt *(Ivan)*; Anthony Warde *(Rogan)*; Stanley Price *(Tonata)*; Frank Lackteen *(Nagoo)*; Stephen Carr *(Tom MacGraw)*.

CLEO AND DON MCGUIRE.

STORY: Congo Bill, a wild animal and jungle expert, undertakes to deliver a letter to Ruth Culver, heiress to the Culver Circus fortune, missing in Africa. There, he learns of the rumored existence of a white queen in the jungle. His safari is beset by many dangers including the henchmen of Andre Bocar, African trader, secretly in league with Bernie McGraw, who hopes to inherit the fortune himself.

CHAPTER I — *The Untamed Beast.*

Tom and Bernie MacGraw, co-managers of the Culver Circus and administrators of a $500,000 trust fund, have been holding the money for any surviving heir of Les Culver, original founder of the show, who, with his party, mysteriously disappeared in Africa almost twenty years ago. Culver's daughter, Ruth, a baby at the time, was among those vanished. According to the trust terms, the MacGraw's will acquire the money unless an heir appears within the next year. Tom tells Bernie he has heard from Andre Bocar, a trader in Icala, Africa, of the rumoured existence of a white queen in the interior. He plans an expedition there. Bernie tries to eliminate his brother by clubbing him into unconsciousness and dragging him close to the cage of a dangerous gorilla. Congo Bill, wild animal trainer and jungle specialist, rushes to the rescue but is waylaid by two assailants.

CHAPTER 2 — *Jungle Gold.*

Congo Bill's attackers are frightened off and he continues to the aid of badly injured Tom. Before Tom dies, he asks Bill to find Ruth Culver, the missing heiress, if at all possible. Bernie and his accomplice, Morelli, expert knife-thrower, hurls a knife at a man thought to be Bill standing on the bridge. The figure falls to his death.

CHAPTER 3 — *A Hot Reception.*

The man killed turns out to be a circus watchman. Bernie sends Bill to Africa after wild animals and wires Bocar to have him disposed of when he arrives. Bill meets a man who has information on the Culver expedition. But the man is murdered, and two of Bocar's men trap Bill as he searches for evidence.

CHAPTER 4 — *Congo Bill Springs a Trap.*

Congo Bill is saved by an unseen man. Bill heads his safari toward the forbidden valley of Namu to look for the mysterious white queen; he chooses a youth, Kahla, as his gun bearer. Bocar's men speed past the group, shooting indiscriminately. Bill and Kahla race after them, when suddenly their car is caught in an explosion.

CHARLES KING, DON MCGUIRE AND CLEO.

CHAPTER 5 — *White Shadows in the Jungle.*

The uninjured Bill rescues Kahla from the wreck. As the safari pushes closer to the forbidden land, Lureen the white queen of Namu Valley, orders Tonata to capture the white man. The witch doctor Nagoo, tells Tonata to kill the whole group, lest they learn of his illicit gold shipments to Bocar. Bill and Kahla are attacked by Tonata; Kahla stumbles and, as Bill bends to help him, a huge rock falls.

CHAPTER 6 — *The White Queen.*

Congo Bill pulls Kahla to safety as the boulder hurtles by. The mysterious stranger chases off the pursuing tribesmen. Soon afterwards, Lureen's lion attacks Bill and, when she tends his wounds in her tent, Bill discovers that she is Ruth Culver. Tonata and Nagoo plan to sacrifice Bill. Threatened from all sides, Bill and Lureen attempt to cross a quicksand swamp.

CHAPTER 7 — *Black Panther.*

The stranger and Kahla save Bill and Lureen from the quicksand. She remains with her tribe, while Bill continues the search for the stolen Culver letter. Kahla, serving as a lookout while Bill ransacks Bocar's house for the letter, is knocked out by Bocar's henchmen. Bill escapes capture.

CLEO AND DON MCGUIRE.

Kahla revives but springs a trap which throws him into a pit containing a wild black panther.

CHAPTER 8 — *Sinister Schemes.*
Congo Bill saves Kahla from the panther. Bernie and Morelli arrive from the States. Meanwhile, Bill is captured and placed under an elaborate torture mechanism. Attempting his rescue, Kahla is knocked out and Bill moves steadily closer to revolving knife blades and certain death.

CHAPTER 9 — *The Witch Doctor Strikes.*
Bill is saved by the stranger, Bocar, seeking to make peace with Bill, proposes that Congo Bill head a new safari organized for Bernie. Bill decides to play along. Tonata's tribesmen attack them and Nagoo promises not to harm them but asks that the expedition take back to Bocar's certain goods, really gold he is smuggling. Bill is captured when he trails Nagoo to a sacred temple. Bowmen string their arrows and let fly.

CHAPTER 10 — *Trail of Treachery.*
Bill escapes death when Kahla topples a stone idol I the path of the arrows. Nagoo agrees to commute the death sentence. The expedition leaves for Icala, carrying the concealed gold. Bocar plans to highjack the safari at night to obtain the gold, but Lureen sees him and is seized. Attempting to free Lureen, Bill is caught in a noose. Congo Bill is hanging helplessly, head down, when a Bocar man fires at the hanging figure, which suddenly goes limp.

CHAPTER 11 — *A Desperate Chance.*
Having only pretended to be hit, Bill frees himself and releases Lureen. Cameron, the mysterious stranger, and Kahla are captured at Bocar's hideout. Congo Bill goes after his friends. Kahla, who has escaped, intercepts Bill and leads him to Cameron. Bernie and Morelli knock out Kahla, then overpower Bill and Cameron, rendering them unconscious. A fire sets off some nearby explosive.

CHAPTER 12 — *The Lair of the Beast.*
Congo Bill regains consciousness a few moments before the explosion and drags Cameron to safety. Kahl manages to join them. Lureen decides to return to Namu and see that the witch doctor is punished; she is captured by Nagoo. Congo Bill's party splits in two in the jungle, and Cameron is captured by Nagoo's tribesmen. Nagoo hypnotizes Cameron into attempting to stab Bill.

WHITE SHADOWS
IN THE JUNGLE
Chapter 5
CONGO BILL
King of the Jungle
A COLUMBIA SERIAL
By Arrangement with National Comics Publications, Inc.

MENACE OF
THE JUNGLE
Chapter 13
CONGO BILL
King of the Jungle
A COLUMBIA SERIAL
By Arrangement with National Comics Publications, Inc.

CHAPTER 13 — *Menace of the Jungle.*
Cameron only pretends to kill Congo Bill because he's watched by Nagoo, who has followed him. Bill and his friends rescue Lureen. Bocar kills Nagoo, and then, with his allies, heads back for Icala. Bernie and Bocar quarrel over the gold and there's a split between the two factions. Bernie and Morelli try to eliminate Lureen by letting a gorilla into her room.

CHAPTER 14 — *Treasure Trap.*
Congo Bill arrives in time to save Lureen from being killed. Two of Bill's friends are captured by Bocar men and are taken to Bocar's hideout to be questioned. Congo Bill and Kahla follow and free the prisoners, whom Bocar has tied up in the hot sun to loosen their tongues. Bill starts out to locate the hiding place of the gold. He is caught in a deadly trap, while one of Bocar's men stands by to prevent rescue.

CHAPTER 15 — *The Missing Letter.*
Bill is saved by Cameron, but the small party is trapped with the arrival of additional Bocar men. Bocar sets off a blast by remote control but destroys only his own men. Bocar is seized, and Cameron, taking charge of him, reveals himself as a member of Colonial Intelligence working on the theft

of the gold, which was stolen from the government. Bernie and Morelli seize Congo Bill and Lureen but Bill manages to free himself and subdue his enemies. Bill and Lureen leave for the States, promising a bigger circus than ever.

NOTES: April 28, 1948, marked the start of filming for Don McGuire and Cleo Moore. May 15, 1948, Mexican actress Armida and character actor Charles King were signed to take part in *Congo Bill*. In June, Hugh Prosser and I. Stanford Jolley were signed by producer Sam Katzman, for the two principal heavy roles.

Congo Bill was largely shot on location at Thousand Oaks, Ventura County, CA. The serial was released on October 28, 1948.

Don McGuire was injured by an arrow during the filming of a sequence in which Congo Bill is ambushed. McGuire was to hide behind a rock while the natives shot poison arrows at him. One of the arrows, rubber-tipped and fired by a special effects man, glanced of the rock. The tip fell off and the wooden shaft struck McGuire on the forehead, directly between the eyes. The wound required four stitches.

Congo Bill is a quite boring film serial based on a DC Comics series. The African landscape is very recognizable as California, and the tribe Cleo rules are dressed like Polynesians instead of African tribesman. The serial was aimed for the typical 8-year-old who could enjoy this piece of hokum.

Cleo makes her entry in episode five, "White Shadows in the Jungle." She orders her tribesmen to bring back Congo Bill and his mates to her for questioning.

Don McGuire (1919-1999) was a former Warner Brothers contract player. One of his first assignments after leaving WB was *Congo Bill*. McGuire found good roles hard to come by and he ended up playing in second features. He eventually turned screenwriter and director. McGuire wrote and directed *Hear Me Good* (1957) and he co-wrote the original story of *Tootsie* (1982). Some of McGuire's other films, are: *My Wild Irish Rose* (1947) and *Sideshow* (1950).

When she was eighteen-year-old, Mexican-born Armida (1911-1989), was offered a five-year contract at Warner Brothers. She showed promise as the gypsy bride of John Barrymore in *General Crack* (1929). At Universal she played with Maria Montez in *South of Tahiti* (1941). Poverty Row studio PRC tried to create their own 'Mexican Spitfire' when they cast her in *The Girl from Monterrey* (1943). Singing and dancing in films kept her busy but didn't make her into a 'new Lupe Velez.' *Congo Bill* was one of her last movie assignments.

JOE MCDOAKES SHORTS

Cleo was cast in three episodes of the popular Warner Bros. short comedies, *Behind the Eight Ball*. The series involved 'Mister Average' Joe McDoakes, an anti-hero played by George O'Hanlon. The character's name comes from 'Joe Doakes,' which was a slang term for the average man.

Her first appearance is the one that features her the best, she has a couple of close-ups and enough dialogue throughout the movie. In *So You're Having In-Law Trouble*, Cleo plays George's cousin, Ellie Mae. Ellie Mae is an orphan girl George's parents raised. She's a floozie, immediately kissing George on the mouth by their introduction and their goodbye. In *So You Want to Be an Actor*, she's an actress, Scarlett, a Southern Belle. She's seen for a couple of minutes in a scene were Joe ruins the play they are in. Her last appearance is a mere cameo. Dressed in the same black and white striped sweater and black skirt as *So You Want to Be an Actor*, she plays a party guest, Mrs Frisbee, in *So You Want to Throw a Party*.

SO YOU'RE HAVING IN-LAW TROUBLE
1949 — Warner Bros.
10 minutes — Black and White

SO YOU WANT TO BE AN ACTOR
1949 — Warner Bros.
11 minutes — Black and White

SO YOU WANT TO THROW A PARTY
1950 — Warner Bros.
10 minutes — Black and White

711 OCEAN DRIVE
1950 — Columbia
102 minutes — Black and White

DIRECTOR: Joseph M. Newman. PRODUCER: Frank N. Seltzer. SCREEN-PLAY: Francis Swann and Richard English. PHOTOGRAPHY: Frank F. Planer. MUSIC: Sol Kaplan. EDITING: Bert Jordan. SOUND: James Gaither. MAKEUP: Jack Byron. HAIR: Ann Locker. COSTUMES: Odette

Myrtil. ART DIRECTION: Perry Furgeson. SET DECORATION: Howard Bristol.

CAST: Edmond O'Brien *(Mal Granger)*; Joanne Dru *(Gail Mason)*; Otto Kruger *(Carl Stephans)*; Barry Kelley *(Vince Walters)*; Dorothy Patrick *(Trudy Maxwell)*; Donald Porter *(Larry Mason)*; Howard St. John *(Lieutenant Pete Wright)*; Robert Osterloh *(Gizzi)*; Sammy White *(Chippie Evans)*; Jay Barney *(Detective Carter)*; Bert Freed *(Steve Marshak)*; Joe Gray *(Boxer)*; Carl Milletaire *(Joe Gish)*; **Cleo Moore** *(Mal's Date)*; Gail Bonney *(Chippie's Date)*.

STORY: Edmond O'Brien plays a telephone repairman who uses his knowledge to help his bookie expand his business to increased profits and rises to the top. But when syndicate head Otto Kruger wants to take over, things start to get dicey and O'Brien's in too deep to call the cops.

REVIEWS: Despite some considerable advertising of *711 Ocean Drive* as a daring and courageous revelation of the big bookmaking and gambling syndicates, this modest Columbia melodrama, which came to the

CLEO AND EDMOND O'BRIEN.

Paramount yesterday, is no more than an average crime picture with some colorful but vague details thrown in. Certainly no one who reads the papers with a fairly retentive eye can have any less comprehension of the gambling racket than is illustrated here…In short, this little picture, conventionally written but well photographed, does no more than any gangster picture in reminding us that gangsters are crooks. (*The New York Times*)

Operations of the syndicates are given a realistic touch by the screenplay, and Joseph M. Newman's direction keeps action at a fast pace. O'Brien is excellent as the hot-tempered, ambitious young syndicate chief. (*Variety*)

Its story about the rise of an aggressive telephone repair man to a big-time bookie is not pleasant, for it involves cheating, blackmail and murder, yet it grips one's attention because of the graphic way in which it exposes the tricks and devices employed in the bookie racket, and the cunning but illegal manner in which wire services furnish the bookies with information on horse races from the tracks. (*Harrison's Reports*)

NOTES: Director Joseph Newman said: "it was tremendously successful picture. It was a picture that got good reviews and the studios all liked it. After that picture I was in great demand." It led to him working at 20th Century-Fox for two years and directing Marilyn Monroe in *Love Nest* (1951). Newman also directed *The Human Jungle* (1954) with Jan Sterling, science-fiction classic *This Island Earth* (1954) and *The George Raft Story* (1961) with Jayne Mansfield and Barbara Nichols.

711 Ocean Drive was released on July 4, 1950.

Cleo shares her one scene with Edmond O'Brien (1915-1985). O'Brien made his Broadway debut in 1936, appearing in *Hamlet* and *Romeo and Juliet*, in the following years. RKO brought him to Hollywood where he landed himself a supporting part in *The Hunchback of Notre Dame* (1939). He married and divorced actresses Nancy Kelly and Olga San Juan. Memorable performances are: *The Killers* (1946), *D.O.A.* (1949), *The Hitch-Hiker* (1953) and *The Girl Can't Help It* (1956), with Jayne Mansfield.

BRIGHT LEAF

1950 — Warner Bros.
110 minutes — Black and White

DIRECTOR: Michael Curtiz. PRODUCER: Henry Blanke. SCREENPLAY:
Ranald McDougall, based on the novel by Foster Fitzsimmons.
PHOTOGRAPHY: Karl Freund. MUSIC: Victor Young. EDITING: Owen
Marks. SOUND: Stanley Jones. MAKEUP: Perc Westmore, Ray Romero,
John Wallace. HAIR: Myrl Stoltz. COSTUMES: Marjorie Best, Leah
Rhodes. ART DIRECTION: Stanley Fleischer. SET DECORATION: Ben
Bone.

CAST: Gary Cooper *(Brant Royle)*; Lauren Bacall *(Sonia Kovac)*; Patricia
Neal *(Margaret Jane Singleton)*; Jack Carson *(Chris Malley/Dr. Monaco)*;
Donald Crisp *(Major James Singleton)*; Gladys George *(Rose)*; Elizabeth
Patterson *(Tabitha Singleton)*; Jeff Corey *(John Barton)*; Taylor Holmes
(Lawyer Calhoun); Thurston Hall *(Phillips)*; Marietta Canty *(Sonia's maid
Queenie)*; James Griffith *(Ellery)*; Celia Lovsky *(Dressmaker)*; Nita Talbot

CLEO, GLADYS GEORGE, DENNIS MORGAN AND LAUREN BACALL.

(Cousin Emily); **Cleo Moore** *(Cousin Louise);* Renee De Vaux *(Cousin Pearl);* Irmgard Dawson *(Bridesmaid).*

STORY: Brant Royle returns to Kingsmont. Only one person, Sonia Kovac, is happy over his return. She loves him, but Royle is determined to wed Margaret Jane Singleton, whose tobacco tycoon father had him banished from the town. Royle forms a cigarette company, rises to wealth and power, breaks Margaret's dad and forces her to marry him. She gets revenge by ruining him. Although Sonia's bitter over Royle's rejection of her, she still loves him and goes to him when he needs her. When Royle learns about the betrayal of his wife that leaves him bankrupt, he evicts her from their mansion, sets fire to it and lets it burn to the ground. He then returns to Sonia. She tells him that she lost all feelings for him and he rides off a dejected man.

REVIEWS: And the fault of *Bright Leaf* as a drama of a greedy man thwarted in love, is that it runs too much to the conventional and is too insufferably long. The screenplay by Ranald MacDougall is a literate piece of writing, with a couple of taut dramatic scenes, but virtually every twist in it can be seen a mile away. Furthermore, although Mr. Cooper does a commendably strong and vivid job as a man wracked by agitating passions which propel him to his doom, Patricia Neal plays his female tormentor as though she were some sort of vagrant lunatic. *(New York Times)*

The first-rate production values given to this adaption of Foster Fitz-Simon's novel, and its colorful depiction of the growth of the tobacco industry in the late 1890's, make it a striking picture in many respects. On the whole, however, it is no more than a fairly interesting drama that will have to depend on the drawing power of its players. Adult in dialogue and in treatment, the picture is overlong, plot-heavy and slow-paced, and its theme of love and revenge somewhat unpleasant. *(Harrison's Report)*

NOTES: The town of Kingsmont, presumably in North Carolina, was built completely by Warner Bros on the Calabanas ranch, 30 miles from the studio. Lauren Bacall's 'rooming house for ladies' was built completely from scratch for this picture.

While filming *Bright Leaf,* Cleo's thirteen-year-old sister Mary Lea became very ill. Cleo's parents took her to a doctor, who told her she had a tumor, and she had a 2% chance to survive. "We arranged for the operation, and I had to go to the studio, where I was working in a Gary Cooper movie.

I kept thinking what the doctor had said. I started to become hysterical, and Cooper noticed it. He came over and asked me what was wrong. I told him that my sister was, practically at that very moment, on the operating table." A religious man, Gary Cooper told Cleo that he would pray for her little sister. "He disappeared into his dressing room, and I felt a bit better, although I could not stop crying." Finally, the doctor called and told Cleo that they removed a ten-pound tumor. "Later I was told that Mary Lea had gone into shock and was kept in an airlock, and the operation took three hours! Yes, it was completely successful. It was indeed a miracle!"[20]

Bright Leaf was released on July 2, 1950.

Gary Cooper (1901-1961) was born in the United States from English parents. His father sent him to boarding school in England. He was an excellent horseman and started his career as an extra in silent western movies. Under contract at Paramount, he was teamed with Marlene Dietrich. He died from cancer, sixty-years-old.

Lauren Bacall (1924-2014) was born in New York City to Polish Jewish parents. She met Humphrey Bogart on the set of her first movie, *To Have and Have Not* (1944) and married him a year later. Together they appeared in *The Big Sleep* (1946), *Dark Passage* (1947) and *Key Largo* (1948). She retired from acting in the movies after her husband died from lung cancer in 1957. Bacall moved back to New York and appeared on the Broadway stage. In 1964 she made her comeback in Hollywood. She was married to actor Jason Robards from 1961 to 1969.

THE GREAT JEWEL ROBBER

1950 — Warner Bros.
91 minutes — Black and White

DIRECTOR: Peter Godfrey. PRODUCER: Bryan Foy. SCREENPLAY: Borden Chase. PHOTOGRAPHY: Sidney Hickox. MUSIC: William Lava. EDITING: Frank Magee. SOUND: Leslie G. Hewitt. MAKEUP: Perc Westmore and Larry Butterworth. HAIR: Agnes Flanagan. ART DIRECTION: Stanley Fleischer. SET DIRECTION: G.W. Berntsen. SCRIPT SUPERVISOR: Rita Michaels.

CAST: David Brian *(Gerard Graham Dennis)*; Marjorie Reynolds *(Martha Rollins)*; John Archer *(Police Detective Lou Sampter)*; Jacqueline deWit

20. *Modern Screen* magazine.

(Mrs. Arthur Vinson); Perdita Chandler *(Peggy Arthur);* Stanley Church *(himself, Mayor of New Rochelle);* Alice Talton *(Brenda Hall);* Claudia Barrett *(Marian Blaine);* Dimples Cooper *(Chinese Girl);* **Cleo Moore** *(Blonde girlfriend);* Herschel Daugherty *(Sergeant Tarrant);* Warren Douglas *(Detective Altman);* Bess Flowers *(Party Guest);* Harold Miller *(Party Guest);* Fred Graham *(Brad Morrow);* Sheilah Graham *(herself, Television Commentator);* Harry Lauter *(Reporter).*

STORY: Escaping from a Canadian prison farm, master thief Gerard Dennis (David Brian) makes his way to Buffalo with Peggy Arthur (Perdita Chandler), who supplies him with money needed for forged papers. Dennis, Peggy and a crooked bartender in a Buffalo hotel pull a robbery in which Dennis is almost caught, but he escapes to find his accomplices have deserted him. Later, confronting them, he is badly beaten and is taken to a hospital where he meets nurse Martha Rollins (Marjorie Reynolds), who falls in love with him. They go to New Rochelle where he is wounded attempting another robbery. Martha performs the necessary surgery, believing that he will give up his life of crime. When she finds him in New York with another girl, Martha gives the police

CLEO, DAVID BRIAN AND JOHN ARCHER.

his picture and hideout location, but he escapes the police trap. He flees to Los Angeles where he meets wealthy divorcee Mrs. Arthur Vinson (Jacqueline De Wit), whose confidence he wins in order to systematically rob her society friends' jewels. He is caught attempting to dispose of the jewels, escapes and in a final chase, nabbed about to board a plane with another blonde (Cleo Moore).

REVIEWS: With David Brian in the top role, the short but exciting career of the society thief as portrayed on the screen becomes a string of second-story jobs, sordid romances and hairbreadth escapes, with the repetition and the knowledge of the thief's ultimate fate softening the film's impact. Some of the scenes are engrossing and highly suspenseful, others are so ineptly handled that one wonders whether the same director worked in them. (*Film Bulletin*)

A fairly interesting crook melodrama, supposedly biographical of the criminal career of Gerard Dennis, the widely publicized thief, who is now serving a prison term of eighteen years. Dennis, effectively played by David Brian, is shown as a suave crook who used many women as dupes to further his schemes. Although it is supposed to be based on fact, the story follows a conventional line for pictures of this type, and offers little that is unusual, but it manages to hold one's interest fairly well since it moves along at a fast and somewhat exciting pace. (*Harrison's Reports*)

NOTES: *The Great Jewel Robber* was also known as *After Nightfall*. Filming was completed September 1949, but the movie was not released until July 15, 1950.

David Brian (1914-1993) signed a contract with Warner Brothers in 1949. *Intruder in the Dust* (1950), earned him a Golden Globe nomination as Best Supporting Actor. He was teamed up with Joan Crawford in several films. Brian was mostly typecast as ruthless or manipulating types. Before David Brian and actress Adrian Booth were married, Adrian's Beverly Hills apartment was robbed of all her furs and jewelry. The police suspected Gerard Dennis of the robbery but had no evidence to convict him.

PUBLICITY PHOTO.

DYNAMITE PASS

1950 — RKO Radio Pictures Inc.
60 minutes — Black and White

DIRECTOR: Lew Landers. PRODUCER: Herman Schlom. SCREENPLAY: Norman Houston. PHOTOGRAPHY: Nicholas Musuraca. MUSIC: Paul Sawtell and C. Bakaleinikoff. EDITING: Robert Swink. SOUND: John Cass and Clem Portman. MAKEUP: Mel Berns. HAIR: Larry Germain. ART DIRECTION: Albert D'Agostino and Walter E. Keller. SET DECORATION: Jack Mills and Darrell Silvera.

CAST: Tim Holt *(Ross Taylor)*; Lynne Roberts *(Mrs. Mary Madden)*; Richard Martin *(Chito Rafferty)*; Regis Toomey *(Dan Madden)*; Robert Shayne *(Jay Wingate)*; Don C. Harvey *(Missouri, Henchman)*; **Cleo Moore** *(Lulu)*; John Dehner *(Anson Thurber)*; Don Haggerty *(Sheriff in Cliffton)*; Ross Elliot *(Stryker, Henchman)*; Denver Pyle *(Thurber, Henchman)*; Chet Brandenburg *(Barfly)*; Frank Matts *(Townsman)*; Merrill McCormick *(Man in Store)*; Stuart Randall *(Allen, Rancher)*; James Young *(Henchman)*.

STORY: When Ross and Chito ride in town, they are just in time to become involved in a fight between Jay Wingate, who collects heavy tolls for the use of his private road, and a surveyor, Dan Madden, commissioned to build a new road. His wife, Mary, hires the two cowpokes to help them get the wagon carrying the surveying instruments through the toll road. There is a lively gun battle, but they get through. A storekeeper, Anson Thurber, tells Madden the wagon will be safe in his locked barn, but Thurber is secretly in league with Wingate, and during a benefit dance the instruments are stolen. Ross and Chito locate the thieves, and foil Wingate's plan to kill Madden by dynamiting the road just as he drives over it en route to Denver for new instruments. Wingate and Thurber are arrested and the road built.

REVIEWS: There are two factors that distinguish — however so slightly — this from the countless predecessors in the series of gallopers starring Tim Holt. The story deviates somewhat from formula oaters and the gal — Lynne Roberts — adds more substance to her role than is usually the case with femme leads in westerns. (*Boxoffice*)

Two gun wearers deliver expertly to continue their fan following. Miss Roberts is an appealing damsel in distress and Toomey comes across capably. Skulduggery is exactly what it should be as projected by Shayne, Dehner and their sundry followers. Cleo Moore is in for a Martin sideline romance, and others measure up. Lew Landers direction keeps it moving and lensing by Nicholas Musuraca is just as actionful. (*Variety*)

Herman Schlom's well-done production supplies a capable cast and some unusually colorful backgrounds in a rock-strewn pass, and Nicholas Musuraca photographs both the action and the scenery very effectively.

CLEO WITH TIM HOLT BEHIND THE SCENES.

Director Lew Landers makes skillful use of a good cast and well-written script to turn out an interesting and fast-moving picture. The film has an unusually good part for the feminine lead, and Lynne Roberts' outstanding performance as the attractive but determined young wife of a surveyor gives extra interest to the piece. Tim Holt gives a manly and convincing performance, and Richard Martin plays his pal efficiently and furnishes some amusing comedy, with Cleo Moore as his partner in a brief romance. (*Hollywood Reporter*)

NOTES: The movie was filmed as *Dynamite Trail*, between September 13 and late September 1949. *Dynamite Pass* was released on March 17, 1950. (Alternative date: June 15, 1950).

Some scenes were shot in Lone Pine, Ca. Cleo's scenes were shot on the Western Street at the RKO ranch in Encino, and on the RKO soundstage in Hollywood.

Dynamite Pass was hailed as one of the best in the series. "The latest Tim Holt starrer, *Dynamite Pass*, is one of the best of the series to date, because it has an interesting and novel plot that is carefully developed with clear

LOBBY CARD, WITH RICHARD MARTIN.

motivations for the action, and avoids most of the conventional western situations"[21]

Tim Holt (1918-1973) was the son of actor Jack Holt. Holt's father appeared in hundreds of silent and talkies over the years. In *The Arizona Ranger* (1948) both men appeared together as father and son. Tim Holt had made his film debut in his father's *The Vanishing Pioneer* (1928). Holt carved out a nice career, working at RKO. WWII interrupted his thriving film career, which he picked up in 1946. Together with his sidekick Richard Martin, Holt appeared in a string of westerns at RKO. He was ranked in the top-ten of money-making cowboy stars during the 1940s and early 1950s. Besides many westerns he starred in several A-budget movies: *Swiss Family Robinson* (1940), *The Magnificent Ambersons* (1942), *Hitler's Children* (1943), and played Humphrey Bogart's prospecting pal in *The Treasure of the Sierra Madre* (1948).

RIO GRANDE PATROL

1950 — RKO Radio Pictures Inc.
60 minutes — Black and White

DIRECTOR: Lesley Selander. PRODUCER: Herman Schlom. SCREENPLAY: Norman Houston. PHOTOGRAPHY: J. Roy Hunt. MUSIC: Paul Sawtell and C. Bakaleinikoff. EDITING: Desmond Marquette. SOUND: John Cass and Clem Portman. MAKEUP: Mel Berns. HAIR: Annabell Levy. ART DIRECTION: Albert D'Agostino and Feild Gray. SET DECORATION: Jack Mills and Darrell Silvera.

CAST: Tim Holt *(Kansas Jones)*; Jane Nigh *(Sherry Bliss)*; Richard Martin *(Chito Jose Gonzales Bustamante Rafferty)*; Douglas Fowley *(Bragg Orket)*; **Cleo Moore** *(Peppie)*; Rick Vallin *(Captain Alberto Trevino)*; John Holland *(Fowler)*; Tom Tyler *(Chet Yance)*; Larry Johns *(Dr. Reynolds)*; Harry Harvey *(Station Master)*; Forest Burns *(Henchman)*; Bob Reeves *(Henchman)*; Clint Sharp *(Henchman)*; Chet Brandenburg *(Bartender)*; Bob Burrows *(Townsman)*.

STORY: Kansas Jones and Chito Rafferty, officers in the U.S. Border Patrol, are sent to Laredo to aid Captain Trevino of the Mexican Rurales in preventing gun-smuggling. Fowler, a dance hall owner, is working

21. *Hollywood Reporter*, March 17, 1950.

with two gun-runners, Orket and Yance. Saloon singer Sherry Bliss tells Captain Trevino that Fowler is bringing in four new girls, and the men plan to search their baggage. But Orket shoots up the train, wounds Trevino, and lures Kansas Jones and Chito away while Fowler hides the guns. Fowler moves his show to another town. Kansas Jones follows, is captured, but his horse brings Chito and Captain Trevino to the rescue. They find the smugglers moving the guns, start a desperate fight and Captain Trevino and the Rurales arrive just in time to capture the crooks.

REVIEWS: Lesley Selander's competent direction does justice to a good script, gives Tim Holt and Richard Martin plenty of opportunities to show their acting abilities, and turns out a film that holds interest throughout. Holt gives a good and vigorous performance, while Martin does a swell job with his well-timed comedy. Miss Nigh acts and sings well as the femme lead, and Cleo Moore wins laughs as a dancing girl. Vallin is well cast as the Captain of the Rurales, while Fowley, Tyler and Holland are proper villains. (*Hollywood Reporter*)

Lesley Selander's direction of the Norman Houston script is actionful in sending the players through their paces. Jane Nigh handles the femme lead nicely as Vallin's betrothed and singer in Holland's saloon. Cleo Moore, showgirl, adds another romance touch with Martin. Fowley and Holland are properly villainous for the western market, with Tom Tyler giving them an assist on the skullduggery. Herman Schlomm smartly sets up the production, the only flaw being the aimless shooting that occurs too often in this oater series. (*Variety*)

NOTES: *Rio Grande Patrol* was released on October 21, 1950. Filming had started on May 17 and was completed on May 26, 1950.

JANE NIGH AND SHOWGIRLS.

Exteriors for the film were shot in Little Rock, in California's Mojave Desert.

Tim Holt's sidekick, Richard Martin (1917-1994), started working in the movie business as a receptionist at MGM in the late 1930s. While under contract at RKO he created the character of Chito Jose Gonzales Bustamante Rafferty, the Irish-Mexican comic sidekick of Holt. Martin grew up in West Hollywood where he learned he could do a very good Spanish accent, having a lot of Hispanic friends. In the early 1950s Martin retired from the movie business.

Blonde Jane Nigh (1925-1993) was a 20th Century-Fox contract player in the 1940s. She found fame, freelancing in B-movies in the 1950s. Several of the movies she appeared in are: *Red, Hot and Blue* (1949), *County Fair* (1950), *Fort Osage* (1952) and *Hold That Hypnotist* (1957) with the Bowery Boys.

HUNT THE MAN DOWN
1951 — RKO Radio Pictures Inc.
69 minutes — Black and White

DIRECTOR: George Archainbaud. PRODUCER: Lewis J. Rachmil. SCREENPLAY: DeVallon Scott. PHOTOGRAPHY: Nicholas Musuraca. MUSIC: Paul Sawtell and C. Bakaleinikoff. EDITING: Samuel E. Beetley. SOUND: Phil Brigandi and Clem Portman. MAKEUP: Mel Berns. ART DIRECTION: Albert S. D'Agostino and Walter E. Keller. SET DECORATION: James Altwies and Darrell Silvera.

CAST: Gig Young *(Paul Bennett)*; Lynne Roberts *(Sally Clark)*; Mary Anderson *(Alice McGuire/Peggy Linden)*; Willard Parker *(Burnell 'Brick' Appleby)*; Carla Balenda *(Rolene Wood)*; Gerald Mohr *(Walter Long)*; James Anderson *(Richard Kincaid aka William H. Jackson)*; John Kellogg *(Kerry 'Lefty' McGuire)*; Harry Shannon *(Wallace Bennett)*; **Cleo Moore** *(Pat Sheldon)*; Christy Palmer *(Joan Brian)*; Iris Adrian *(Marie)*; Vince Barnett *(Joe)*; Ray Walker *(Mac)*; Mira McKinney *(Rolene's aunt)*; Al Hill *(Pete Floogle)*; William Haade *(Bart)*; Paul Frees *(Packard 'Packy' Collins)*; Charles J. Conrad *(Crook)*.

STORY: James Anderson plays a man who is charged with murder although he is innocent. He has escaped from custody during his trial and evaded capture for twelve years. Picked up by the police, he is assigned

Gig Young as his counsel. Anderson tells Young that on the night of the murder he had struck up an acquaintance in a cocktail bar with Carla Balenda and Gerald Mohr; John Kellogg and Mary Anderson; Willard Parker and his fiancée Cleo Moore; and Christy Palmer. All had gone to Kellogg's home. Christy's husband had arrived intoxicated, and he had pulled a gun on Anderson for dancing with her. Later, Christy's husband is found dead. Gig Young sets out to locate the seven witnesses. He finds Parker, now blind from war wounds, mourning Cleo, whom he believed to be dead. Kellogg, now a drunkard, had separated from Mary. Mohr had married Christy. Carla, Cleo's former roommate, had become insane. In a lucid moment, Carla claims to know who had committed the murder, but she is in no condition to testify. Later, Kellogg is shot dead by two gangsters who prove to be associates of Paul Frees, a racketeer. By chance, Young learns that Cleo is not dead, but is married to Frees. He brings the case to trial and calls Cleo to the stand. She successfully wards off Young's attempts to pin the guilt on her, but, when Young has Carla brought into the courtroom, Cleo, thinking that Carla had regained her mind and is waiting to denounce her, confesses that she had killed Christy's first husband because he was blackmailing her.

REVIEWS: The quest for witnesses for a crime 12 years old has novel facets, and holds the attention, because it is well carried out. Lewis J. Rachmil produced the picture, and principal parts are played by Gog Young as the public defender, Lynne Roberts; James Anderson as the man wrongfully accused of murder, Willard Parker; Carla Balenda, very effective; Gerald Mohr; Harry Shannon, who makes much of a good break; Cleo Moore, John Kellogg and others. Nearly all members of the cast have important scenes and were well directed by George Archainbaud. (*L.A. Times*)

Routine rescue number wherein an innocent man is saved and the guilty individual is found out. Lacks fresh approach, novelty. Performances are run of the mill, undistinguished and, in minor cases, unrestrained. (*The Film Daily*)

A moderately interesting program murder mystery melodrama, centring around the efforts of a public defender to clear an innocent man charged with murder. Given more to talk than to action, the picture drags along at a slow pace, despite a spur of excitement here and there, and, even though the guilty person is not uncovered until the closing sequences, the story is so complicated that one's interest in the proceedings wanes. The direction and acting are fair, and the production values modest. (*Harrison's Reports*).

NOTES: Filmed under its working title *Seven Witnesses*, in May. *Hunt the Man Down* was released on December 26, 1950.

Cleo is seen as a brunette in the first part of the movie. She's the missing witness, believed to be deceased. As Geraldine Collins she is called to the witness stand. This time she is no longer a brunette, but a tough blonde.

Supporting actor Gig Young (1913-1978) struggled with alcoholism during his career. He was spotted by Warner Brothers while acting in the play *Pancho* (1941). He served in WWII and asked for his release at WB to freelance. He appeared in *Young at Heart* (1954), *Desk Set* (1957) and *Teacher's Pet* (1958), among others. In 1978, three weeks after marrying German actress Kim Schmidt, Young apparently shot her to death and then turned the gun on himself. Young's Oscar for *They Shoot Horses, Don't They?* (1969) was found near the bodies.

CLEO AND GIG YOUNG.

GAMBLING HOUSE

1951 — RKO Radio Pictures Inc.
80 minutes — Black and White

DIRECTOR: Ted Tetzlaff. PRODUCER: Warren Duff. SCREENPLAY: Marvin Borowsky and Allen Rivkin based on a story by Erwin Gelsey. PHOTOGRAPHY: Harry J. Wild. MUSIC: Roy Webb. EDITING: Roland Gross. SOUND: Phil Brigandi and Clem Portman. MAKEUP: Mel Berns. COSTUMES: Michael Woulfe. ART DIRECTION: Albert S. D'Agostino and Alfred Herman. SET DIRECTION: Jack Mills and Darrell Silvera.

CAST: Victor Mature *(Marc Fury)*; Terry Moore *(Lynn Warren)*; William Bendix *(Joe Farrow)*; Zachary A. Charles *(Willie)*; Basil Ruysdael *(Judge Ravinek)*; Donald Randolph *(Lloyd Crane)*; Damian O'Flynn *(Ralph Douglas)*; **Cleo Moore** *(Sally)*; Ann Doran *(Della)*; Eleanor Audley *(Mrs. Livingston)*; Gloria Winters *(B.J. Warren)*; Don Haggerty *(Sharky)*; Betty Underwood *(Showgirl)*; Kirk Alyn *(FBI Man)*; Frank Wilcox *(Mr. Warren)*; Tol Avery *(Adams)*; Forest Burns *(Milkman)*; Albert Cavens *(Court Clerk)*; G. Pat Collins *(Homicide Detective Jenson)*; Loda Halama *(Mrs. Sobieski)*; Leonard Ossetynski *(Mr. Sobieski)*; Sherry Hall *(Robbins)*; Clark Howat *(Nick)*; Wilbur Mack *(Man at Pier)*; Al Murphy *(Cab Driver)*; Jack Shea *(Wally)*.

STORY: A gangster, Joe Farrow, kills a man after a game of craps, then offers gambler Marc Fury a payment of $50,000 if he will take the rap and stand trial. Farrow tries to renege on the money, so Fury steals a ledger with information that could put Farrow behind bars. Fury manages to be acquitted in court, but immigration officers arrest him and take to Ellis Island and threaten to deport him, proving that neither he nor his parents ever become naturalized citizens. Fury slips the ledger into the possession of an immigration social worker, Lynn Warren, then later tracks her down, retrieves the book and tries to begin a romance. Farrow's gunman comes looking for Fury, but ultimately double-crosses his boss. Lynn still isn't sure how she feels about him, but when Fury offers the $50,000 to a family that needs it to remain in America, she finally admires and trusts him.

REVIEWS: Victor Mature gives a sincere performance of the crook turned straight and Terry Moore is pretty as the social worker. William Bendix is splendid as the heavy. In the supporting cast the best performance is the judge of Basil Ruysdael. (*Hollywood Reporter*)

CLEO AND VICTOR MATURE.

Mature and Bendix are acceptably and characteristically virile, but the plot line with which they and the other cast members were supplied is not quite so robust. As concerns the productional mountings, supporting players and other accoutrements the offering measures up to par, but Ted Tetzlaff's direction shows evidence of having been hampered by the frailties of the script. (*Boxoffice*)

NOTES: In late 1949 the project started as *Mr. Whiskers* and was renamed *Alias Mike Fury*. Victor Mature refused to make the movie and was put on suspension by Fox. The script was rewritten and Mature ended up making the film, which was retitled *Gambling House*. The movie was filmed between February 3 and March 13, 1950. Additional scenes were shot between May 8 and May 13, 1950. *Gambling House* was released on January 20, 1951.

Cleo's part of Willie's girlfriend Sally adds nothing to the plot of the movie. She is seen in a total of four scenes with Zachary Charles and Victor Mature. Another scene where Mature comes to her place and she opens the door and makes a telephone call, clad in a negligee, ended on the cutting room floor.

Victor Mature (1913–1999) had dated Cleo when she first arrived in Hollywood. Producer Hal Roach had awarded him with the lead in *One*

Million B.C. (1940) when he had just arrived in Hollywood himself. His handsome face and physique made a star of Mature. Some of his other movies: *I Wake Up Screaming* (1941), *My Darling Clementine* (1946), *Kiss of Death* (1947), *Samson and Delilah* (1949), *The Robe* (1953), *The Egyptian* (1954) and *The Long Haul* (1957).

Terry Moore (1929), on loan from Columbia, was the movie's female lead. She had worked as a teenage model when she landed a contract at 20th Century-Fox in 1940. In 1953 she received an Academy Award nomination for her performance in Paramount's *Come Back, Little Sheba* (1952). Although she did not share any scenes with Cleo, Terry Moore remembered meeting her on the set. "Cleo was a lovely girl and I wished we would have had an opportunity to work together and get to know her better."[22]

CLEO WITH ZACHARY CHARLES AND VICTOR MATURE.

22. Email contact with author.

ON DANGEROUS GROUND

1951 — RKO Radio Pictures Inc.
82 minutes — Black and White

DIRECTOR: Nicholas Ray. PRODUCER: John Houseman and Sid Rogell.
SCREENPLAY: A.I. Bezzerides, based on the novel *Mad With Much Heart*
by Gerald Butler. PHOTOGRAPHY: George E. Diskant. MUSIC: Bernard
Herrmann. EDITING: Ronald Gross. SOUND: Phil Brigandi, Clem
Portman and Harold M. McNiff. MAKEUP: Mel Berns. HAIRDRESSING:
Larry Germain and Josephine Sweeney. ART DIRECTION: Ralph Berger
and Albert S. D'Agostino. SET DECORATION: Harley Miller and Darrell
Silvera. SPECIAL EFFECTS: Harold E. Stine and Jack Lannan.

CLEO, ANTHONY ROSS AND ROBERT RYAN.

CAST: Ida Lupino *(Mary Malden)*; Robert Ryan *(Jim Wilson)*; Ward Bond *(Walter Brent)*; Charles Kemper *(Pop Daly)*; Anthony Ross *(Pete Santos)*; Ed Begley *(Capt. Brawley)*; Ian Wolfe *(Sheriff Carrey)*; Sumner Williams *(Danny Malden)*; Gus Schilling *(Lucky)*; Frank Ferguson *(Willows)* **Cleo Moore** *(Myrna Bowers)*; Olive Carey *(Mrs. Brent)*; Richard Irving *(Bernie Tucker)*; Pat Priest *(Julie Brent)*; Joan Taylor *(Hazel)*; Tracey Roberts *(Peggy Santos)*; Stephen Roberts *(Charlie)*; Vince Barnett *(George)*; G. Pat Collins *(Sgt. Wendell)*; Billy Hammond *(Fred)*; Ruth Lee *(Helen)*; Nestor Paiva *(Bagganierri)*; Joe Devlin *(Bartender)*; Nita Talbot *(Woman in Bar)*; Ken Terrell *(Crook)*; Don Yager *(Town Resident)*.

STORY: While hunting down the killer of a fellow policeman, veteran detective Jim Wilson grows increasingly morose and violent, causing his more even-tempered partners, Bill 'Pop' Daly and Pete Santos, concern. Acting on a tip from a news vendor, Jim goes to see Myrna Bowers, whose boyfriend, Bernie Tucker, is rumored to be a cohort of the suspected murderers. Jim convinces the battered Myrna to reveal Bernie's whereabouts, and after he tracks Bernie down, beats him into betraying his partners. Later, while on patrol, the detectives hear a woman scream and discover Myrna being beaten by two thugs. Jim grabs one of the men and, without thinking, starts to rough him up. The next day, Brawley yells at Jim that he is becoming a liability to the department and assigns him to assist in the investigation of a young woman's murder in the rural north. Joining the manhunt, in snow-covered terrain, Wilson finds himself paired with the victim's father, Walter Brent, who plans to shoot the killer himself. When the two men come upon a cabin occupied by Mary Malden, a blind woman who is also the killer's sister, Wilson's life is changed forever. Mary, a generous and loving person who has cared for her mentally ill brother Danny since the death of their parents, convinces Wilson to protect Danny from Brent. Wilson also promises to get help for Danny if he surrenders to him.

REVIEWS: Supporting parts are expertly fulfilled, each contributing to the interest of the moment. Anthony Ross and Charles Kemper score briefly as fellow detectives in the opening reels; Cleo Moore is colourful as a moll who tips off Ryan while he's seeking a cop killer. (*Variety*)

Although sequences in the screenplay by A.I. Bezzerides mesh too conveniently at times, it is seldom wanting in the type of excitement that makes for good entertainment...Director Nicholas Ray has kept the action moving briskly and there are many good atmospheric touches to the picture, such as murky streets, cheap taverns and snow-blanketed fields. (*Motion Picture Daily*)

Story is shallow, uneven affair...For all the sincere and shrewd direction and the striking outdoor photography, this RKO melodrama fails to traverse its chosen ground. (*N.Y. Times*)

Cleo Moore, one of Southern California's most photographed models, did surprisingly well during her brief appearance as a racketeer's girlfriend. (*Los Angeles Daily News*)

NOTES: The metropolitan scenes were shot in Boston, Massachusetts. For the country locale the entire troupe travelled to Granby, Colorado, 100 miles northwest of Denver, where they worked in cold and snow at 8,500-foot altitude.

Upon Howard Hughes insistence, ten minutes were cut out of the film, and a scene which originally was just before the ending, the assassination of Myrna, was moved to the ending of the first part of the movie. The film

CLEO WITH ROBERT RYAN, ANTHONY ROSS AND CHARLES KEMPER.

was shelved for almost a year, which was not uncommon at RKO. It was released in December 1951.

Ida Lupino (1918-1995) sandwiched her role in *On Dangerous Ground* between two directorial assignments, *Outrage* (1950) and *Hard, Fast and Beautiful* (1951). She also directed the film for several days when Nicholas Ray fell ill. After she left Warner Brothers in 1947, Lupino freelanced and started directing several movies. Several other movies: *High Sierra* (1941), *The Hard Way* (1943), *Devotion* (1946), *Escape Me Never* (1947), *The Bigamist* (1953).

Robert Ryan (1909-1973) was a man of pacifist beliefs, actively campaigning for improved civil rights and he strongly opposed Senator McCarthy's communist witch hunt. Against character he was often cast as a sadistic, vile villain in film noir features. Ryan appeared in: *Tender Comrade* (1943), *Crossfire* (1947), *Act of Violence 1948)*, *Born to be Bad* (1950) and *Clash by Night* (1952) with Marilyn Monroe.

THE PACE THAT THRILLS

1952 — RKO Radio Pictures Inc.
63 minutes — Black and White

DIRECTOR: Leon Barsha. PRODUCER: Lewis J. Rachmil and Sid Rogell. SCREENPLAY: Robert Lee Johnson and DeVallon Scott. PHOTOGRAPHY: Frank Redman. MUSIC: Paul Sawtell. EDITING: Samuel E. Beetley. SOUND: Phil Brigandi and Clem Portman. ART DIRECTION: Albert S. D'Agostino and Walter E. Keller. SET DECORATION: Jack Mills and Darrell Silvera.

CAST: Bill Williams *("Dusty" Dick L. Weston)*; Carla Balenda *(Eve Drake)*; Robert Armstrong *(J. C. Barton)*; Frank McHugh *(Rocket Anderson)*; Steve Flagg *(Chris Rhodes)*; **Cleo Moore** *(Ruby)*; Diane Garrett *(Opal)*; Claudia Drake *(Pearl)*; John Mallory *(Blackie Myers)*; John Hamilton *(Sour puss)*; Robert Hoheisel *(Hogan)*; Donald Nicolaides *(Thomas)*; Don Fera *(Kerrigan)*; Stanley Irons *(Fitzsimmons)*; Eugene Criswell *(Dunne)*; George Dockstader *(Schrader)*; Frank Hagney *(Starter)*; Pattie Chapman, Gerald Pierce, Don House, Bill Knudson *(Spectators)*; Tom Greenway *(Official)*; Ralph Montgomery *(Announcer at Crater Camp)*; Shirley Rickert, Shirley Powell, Nancy Duke *(Girls)*; Erwin Richardson, Bud Wolfe *(Motorcycle officers)*; Don Dillaway *(Clerk)*; Jack Gargan *(Proprietor)*; Donald Kerr *(Carnival men)*; Dorothy Neumann *(Mrs. Anderson)*;

CLEO AND BILL WILLIAMS.

W. J. O'Brien *(Barker)*; Jonni Paris *(Garret)*; Betty Jane Pettit *(Sapphire)*; Charlotte Portney *(Seretary)*.

STORY: When Los Angeles reporter Eve Drake observes top motorcyclist 'Dusty' Dick L. Weston executing what she considers to be dirty tricks during a race, she is shocked and disgusted. Eve, who has been assigned to write a story about motorcycling, refrains from denouncing the womanizing Dusty as she presents him with his trophy, but slaps him when he tries to kiss her. That night, at the home of motorcycle mechanic Rocket Anderson, where Dusty rents a room, Dusty and his best friend, Chris Rhodes, a motorcycle designer, discuss Eve. When Dusty rejects

CLEO, STEVE FLAGG AND DIANE GARRETT.

Chris's suggestion to try to "soften her up," Chris, who finds Eve attractive, decides to do the job himself. To that end, Chris invites Eve to ride on the back of his motorcycle and takes her to Crater Camp, where motorcycle enthusiasts practice trick riding and race one another. Eve is impressed by the skill and energy of the participants and admits to Chris that she may have misjudged the sport. Finally admitting her attraction, Eve agrees to go out with Dusty after the race. During the race, Chris has a comfortable lead over Dusty until his bike's gears suddenly jam, causing him to fall. As Chris attempts to get back on his bike, Dusty deliberately knocks him down, breaking his leg, and goes on to win. Eve angrily condemns Dusty. After Dusty apologizes to Chris, Eve offers Chris her savings so that he can perfect his hydraulic bike on his own. Dusty prepares to leave town, but before going, hears about Eve's sacrifice and asks Rocket to give Chris additional money that he will send back from the road. Dusty then joins the carnival circuit as a trick rider and, with Rocket acting as his front, helps Chris pay for his new design. As work on the bike progresses, Chris and Eve grow close, although Eve still has feelings for Dusty. When Dusty finally returns to town, Chris, who found out about his friend's generosity from Rocket, admits that he is in love with Eve, but knows she does not as yet return his affection. Dusty has a talk with Eve, trying to convince her that Chris is the man for her. After Eve declares her love, however, Dusty also confesses, and the two kiss. Just before the race, Dusty informs Chris that he and Eve are engaged, prompting Chris to slug his friend and enter the race himself. Dusty enters on another bike, and the men battle each other for several laps. As they near the finish, Chris, whose leg is not completely healed, falls in front of Dusty. Abandoning his usual tactics, Dusty falls next to Chris, who remounts and wins the race.

REVIEWS: *The Pace That Thrills* is a mildly diverting motorcycle racing film that should go over fairly well with action fans. Story is unimaginative, but the motor bike background is sufficiently intriguing to keep audiences interested. Williams plays the cocky rider in engaging style. Miss Balenda, a very pretty girl, handles her undemanding role appealingly and competently. Armstrong, Flagg and Frank McHugh all register nicely. (*Hollywood Reporter*)

Lewis J. Rachmil's production wisely makes frequent use of racing footage to keep up the interest. Leon Barsha's direction is okay, as are the other technical elements. (*Variety*)

NOTES: The working title of the movie was *Crack Down*. Several scenes in the picture were shot at Crater Camp near Calabasas, CA. The production date was June 9 — late June 1950. On March 21, 1952 *The Pace That Thrills* was released.

Cleo is seen in the opening scenes of the movie. Entering the scene riding a motorcycle with Dusty. Cheering on Dusty, who loses interest in her as soon as he sees Carla Balenda. Cleo's dialogue isn't anything more than cheering Dusty on while he is racing. Furthermore, she's adjusting her makeup in the race scene, where Carla Balenda is essential to the story and Cleo is not. Further on in the movie, she is seen cheering on Dusty again and playing the jukebox in a joint where Dusty gets in a brawl. Cleo's part is a typical starlet role; sexy decoration.

The Pace That Thrills is filmed from the 1950s male point of view. Williams makes a sexist remark when he is handed the column "A Woman's Angle" written by journalist Carla Balenda. "Woman shouldn't have angles, only curves." In that category fall his groupies, among whom Cleo. They are named after gemstones: Ruby, Opal and Pearl.

RKO contract player Bill Williams (1915-1992) was married to actress Barbara Hale. Appearing mostly in B-movies, he is probably best known for his starring role in the television series *The Adventures of Kit Carson* (1951-1955).

THY NEIGHBOR'S WIFE

1952 — 20th Century-Fox
77 minutes — Black and White

DIRECTOR: Hugo Haas. PRODUCER: Hugo Haas and Robert Erlik. SCENARIO: Hugo Haas, from the novel "The Peasant Judge" by Oscar Jellinek. PHOTOGRAPHY: Paul Ivano. MUSIC: Václav Divina. EDITING: Albert Shaff, Merrill G. White. MAKEUP: Dave Grayson. HAIRDRESSING: Marsha Masha. SOUND: Benny Winkler. COSTUME DESIGNER: Gus Heimo. SCRIPT SUPERVISOR: Arnold Laven. DIALOGUE SUPERVISOR: Mark Lowell.

CAST: Hugo Haas *(Judge Raphael Vojnar)*; **Cleo Moore** *(Lita Vojnar)*; Ken Carlton *(Quirin Michael)*; Kathleen Hughes *(Anushka)*; Anthony Jochim *(Sima)*; Tom Fadden *(Honza Kratky)*; Darr Smith *(bit part)*; Oscar O'Shea *(bit part)*; Tom Wilson *(bit part)*; Roy Engels *(bit part)*; Robert Knapp *(bit part)*; Joe Duval *(bit part)*; Henry Corden *(bit part)*.

 To protect a relative from punishment, Lita had married the middle-aged Raphael Vojnar, ruthless and haughty judge of a Moravian village. She inwardly despises him, and for that reason grasps the opportunity to carry on an affair with Quirin, her irresponsible but handsome ex-sweetheart, who had just returned to the village after a long absence. When Quirin's uncle is murdered, he becomes the chief suspect because of his refusal to explain his whereabouts on the night of the crime. Actually,

CLEO AND KEN CARLTON.

he had spent the night with Lita, while Vojnar was away on business, and he was trying to protect her. To save Quirin, Lita enters into a conspiracy with Anushka, her servant girl, to claim that she was with Quirin on the night of the murder. Lita then uses her womanly wiles to induce her husband to accept the alibi. Later, however, he learns the truth. Insanely jealous, but unwilling to have it known that his wife had made a fool of him, Vojnar sets in motion a plan to railroad Quirin to jail for the murder. But a hitch develops when Honza, the village idiot, comes to the judge's home and confesses that he had committed the murder. To keep Honza quiet, Vojnar murders him and proceeds to frame Quirin for both killings. Lita, who had secretly witnessed the killing, reveals her knowledge to Vojnar when he catches her preparing to run away with Quirin. Enraged, he strangles her to death and ends up on the gallows himself.

REVIEWS: A fair program drama. Set in an early 19th Century European village, it is a somber concoction of infidelity, jealousy and murder, revolving around a ruthless middle-aged judge, whose beautiful young wife carries on a secret affair with her former boyfriend. Although it has been produced, directed and acted with skill, its appeal will be limited, for the

story is cheerless and unpleasant, and lacks human interest. Hugo Haas is impressive as the insanely jealous judge, but neither he nor the other principal characters are sympathetic. The photography is good, but it is in a low key. (*Harrison's Reports*)

A maturity of theme and treatment immediately sets *Thy Neighbor's Wife* off from the routine. The picture is always absorbing and offers some sharp impressions of human nature. Haas gives the role of the magistrate a full-bodied treatment, with Cleo Moore convincingly frightened and confused as his lovely wife. Ken Carlton portrays the lover. (*Motion Picture Daily*)

Twentieth-Fox dug into its vault of independent productions and came out with Hugo Haas' *Thy Neighbor's Wife*. This film should satisfy the particular clan of Haas' followers, but the general audience prospects are somewhat less than bright. The story is of a European flavour, heavily laden with murder and adultery. Unfortunately, the mixture does not quite jell into a polished picture. Hugo Haas as the judge is appropriately menacing and haughty. Cleo Moore is more physical than histrionic. Ken Carlton is passable as the accused killer, and Kathleen Hughes does as well as can be expected with a shallow role of the household maid induced to cover up

CLEO AND HUGO HAAS.

the local goings-on. Tom Fadden, as the town idiot and real killer, is the best of the supporting cast. Haas' production is better than his direction, which in turn is better than his screenplay. Lensing by Paul Ivano is good, and Václav Divina's score conducted by Adolph Heller portrays the desired moods. (*Hollywood Reporter*)

Haas' latest release, *Thy Neighbour's Wife*, is a typical Haas model. Typical, because it offers two firm double-bill bets, an emotional story and a

CLEO AND KEN CARLTON.

glamorous blonde. Cleo Moore provides the glamour — Haas himself provides the rest. He's a Mr.-Do-Everything who writes, produces, directs and stars in all his films. Here, he plays the arrogant civic ruler of a nineteenth-century Moravian village. He's tormented by jealousy when he finds his wife (Cleo Moore) has taken a young farmer as a lover. It's highly coloured emotional intrigue, stripped of sophisticated tricks. Often it gets dangerously near the line where melodrama draws giggles. Haas is a showman who knows his trade. In Cleo Moore, a baby-faced blonde, he has the right foil for his barn-storming style. (*Picturegoer*)

Thy Neighbor's Wife follows the same line as previous Hugo Haas productions, emerging a sombre drama of human conflicts which will have limited appeal, despite the care with which it has been turned out. By its very nature, film is suitable only for fill-in dates in program houses. Haas delivers a powerful characterization of a man insanely in love, and Miss Moore is excellent in a dramatic role. Carlton, a new face, looks to have a future as a romantic actor. Kathleen Hughes, as the servant girl, stands out among the supporting cast, each of whom has been well selected. Technical credits measure up to the acting. Paul Ivano's photography is artistic, Adolph

Heller's direction of the music score is atmospheric and Martin Obzina's art direction expert. (*Variety Daily*)

NOTES: The opening credits contain the following written prologue: "This strange story of sin and evil happened more than one hundred years ago in an old Moravian village…" The year was set 1841 in the village of Skalni Hradec. The opening scene shows us villagers in their Sunday best clothes, leaving church and wandering the village square. The Sunday peace is disrupted by a man who drags his wife to the square where he scaffolds her. The townspeople gather around and call the woman names. The adulteress must be punished by whipping. From her window Lita oversees the action and when her husband, a judge, returns home she tells him to end what's going on outside. The despise Lita shows for her husband when he tells her that women should know their place in life, makes it clear that this is not a happy marriage. Adultery, sadism, betrayal and misfeasance are the ingredients of this little gem. At the end Lita is strangled by the judge. The murder of his wife and his lying about the true murderer of Quirin's uncle eventually brings the judge to the gallows himself. The film ends with a written epilogue stating, "As the whirlwind passeth, so are the wicked no more…" *Proverbs 692–25.*

Although he is not credited onscreen, Arnold Phillips is listed by a February 1951 *Los Angeles Times* news item and a September 1951 *New York Times* article as Haas's collaborator on the film's story. By July 1951, Haas and Phillips had finished the screenplay. Arnold Phillips died a year later.

A *Hollywood Reporter* news items include Dan Barton, Wayne Tredway, Tempe Pigott and Michael Mark in the cast, but their appearance in the completed picture has not been confirmed.

For his third venture, Haas needed an actress with an East European look. With the money he made from the two former productions, he financed *Thy Neighbor's Wife.* In Cleo Hugo found "an American girl who has the right Slavic face." Besides the unknown MGM contract player Kenny Garcia, who was re-named Ken Carlton, Hugo surrounded himself with all the Czech actors he could find, Czech music for the score and a Czech set designer. Carlton was a bit playing actor when he first met Hugo Haas. Hugo liked him and after playing a couple of small parts on TV and in films, Hugo used him again for his film *Edge of Hell* (1956).

Kathleen Hughes (1928) played Cleo's maid. She started out as a starlet at 20th Century-Fox but reached fame at Universal-International where she rivalled Mamie Van Doren as a blonde bombshell. *The Glass*

Web (1953), *It Came from Outer Space* (1954) and *Cult of the Cobra* (1955) are the cult classics she appeared in. When freelancing in the early fifties, Kathleen auditioned for the part of the servant girl. She remembers that the filming was a pleasant experience, and that Cleo was very nice to her. She has nothing but praise for Hugo Haas and loved working on the film. "It was a wonderful experience. I loved him, I miss him. I think I was very lucky to work with him."[23]

Filming started late July 1951 at the Motion Picture Center, for Hugo Haas Productions, Inc. Production was wrapped up in October 1951. The Los Angeles opening was on September 11, 1953.

The National Legion of Decency rated the movie in category B, objecting, "Suggestive situations; tends to create sympathy for wrongdoing."

LOBBY CARD.

23. Source: telephone conversation with author.

STRANGE FASCINATION

1952 — Columbia Pictures
80 minutes — Black and White

DIRECTOR: Hugo Haas. PRODUCER: Hugo Haas and Robert Erlik. SCENARIO: Hugo Haas. PHOTOGRAPHY: Paul Ivano. MUSIC: Adolf Heller. EDITING: Merrill G. White. MAKEUP: Gustaf Norin. SOUND: Victor Appel. COSTUME DESIGNER: Irving Mitzman. SCRIPT SUPERVISOR: Jack Herzberg. DIALOGUE SUPERVISOR: Mark Lowell.

CAST: **Cleo Moore** *(Margo);* Hugo Haas *(Paul Marvan);* Mona Barrie *(Diana Fowler);* Rick Vallin *(Carlo);* Karen Sharpe *(June Fowler);* Marc Krah *(Shiner);* Geneviève Aumont *(Yvette);* Patrick Holmes *(Walter Fowler);* Maura Murphy *(Mary);* Brian O'Hara *(Douglas);* Anthony Jochim *(Investigator);* Frank Hilliard *(Night Club Manager);* Dr. Ross Thompson *(Dr. Thompson);* Maria Bibikov *(Nurse);* Gayne Whitman *(Mr. Lowell);* Roy Engel *(Mr. Frim);* Robert Knapp *(Jack);* Tom Wilson *(Printing Foreman);* Mark Andrews (Bit part).

STORY: Paul Marvan, a famed but penniless European pianist, accepts the offer of Diana Fowler, a wealthy widow, to come to the United States under her sponsorship. The night before his opening in Philadelphia, Marvan, dining in a café, inadvertently disturbs Margo, a dancer. Peeved, she attends his concert with plans to upset him, only to be captivated by his playing. She visits his dressing room after the concert and apologizes for her intentions. They become friends and he takes her out to dinner. Shortly after he returns to his New York apartment after a successful tour, Mary comes to see him and persuades him to take her under his roof to escape possible bodily harm from Carlo, her dance partner, with whom she had split. In the weeks that follow, her youth and sexiness stir his middle-aged libido and he persuades her to marry him. He is happy with her for a while, but he eventually begins to torture himself with jealousy over her past boyfriends. His troubles multiply when a series of concerts that had been arranged for him is cancelled. He soon finds himself penniless and moves to a tawdry apartment. Margo secures employment as a model, but Marvan makes her quit when she starts accepting favors from more and more men. He telephones Diana for a loan, but she, disappointed over his marriage, turns him down. Aware that Margo will leave him unless he can support her in style, Marvan, in desperation, mangles one of his hands in a printing press to collect $50,000 insurance. The insurance company,

PUBLICITY PHOTO WITH HUGO HAAS
AND MONA BARRIE.

however, denies his claim when they obtain proof that the injury was not accidental. Marvan suffers a final blow when Margo leaves him to take up with her former dance partner. He goes completely to pieces, ending up on the Bowery, where he plays the piano with one hand in a Salvation Army center; gathering a new audience.

REVIEWS: Drama is a word that is thrown about rather promiscuously these days. But we feel that *Strange Fascination*, now in Basil's Lafayette Theater, is worthy of the title. Hollywood calls it a "shocker" film. It is written, produced and directed by Hugo Haas, who also plays the central role. It is tense, interesting entertainment. The conclusion is pathetically realistic. Mr. Haas, whose speech has fine timbre, is a truly mature and mellow player. His performance is notable — full of light and shade. A well-etched portrayal of the romantic sponsor is offered by Miss Barrie. Miss Moore's appearance is arresting but her dramatic ability decidedly is limited. (*Buffalo Evening News*)

As in *Pickup* and *The Girl on the Bridge*, his two previous efforts, Hugo Haas has once again undertaken the chores of a writer, producer, director and star of *Strange Fascination*. And he has once again used as his theme the moral disintegration of a middle-age man who becomes involved with a sexy blonde who traps him into marriage. It is a sordid drama, void of humor, best suited for adult audiences who do not mind unpleasant themes. As the middle-aged concert pianist who is reduced to a tawdry existence, Haas tries to win sympathy for himself, but his dilemma does not touch the spectator because he is motivated by lust for a younger woman. Cleo Moore is sex personified as the buxom blonde who inveigles Haas, but her acting can stand improvement. The ending, which finds Haas reduced to the status of a Bowery bum, is depressing. (*Harrison's Reports*)

Written, produced and directed by Hugo Haas, this is a downbeat, depressing, longhair offering with little general audience appeal. Made on a modest production budget, Haas has contrived to give it plenty of atmosphere, but, while his direction has some subtle touches, the dialogue is nothing to write home about. Haas' own performance as the European pianist who falls in love with a cheap little American dancer, who drags him to the gutter, is realistic and convincing enough. Mona Barrie, as his "angel," is also capable and Cleo Moore, the blonde dancer, gives the cameraman the right architectural angles. But the cast has little or no marquee value. One of the highlights of the picture is the music played by Jacob Gimpel, who also composed the nocturne. (*Film Bulletin*)

CLEO, HUGO HAAS AND MARK ANDREWS.

This latest Hugo Haas production is frankly a "shocker" and its best exploitation possibility will lie in emphasis on the charms of Cleo Moore, who plays the sexy dame whose powers of seduction bring about the downfall of the middle-aged and sensitive European composer-pianist, played by Haas. Haas as producer, director, author of the screenplay and star, acquits himself well except for some trite dialog. Miss Moore certainly demonstrates her claim to enrolment in the ranks of the newer exponents of cinematic sin. There is no single light touch to relieve the steady march

CLEO AND HUGO HAAS.

of the film's tragic events and the spectator's realization that things are bad and getting no better fast. Haas' performance is practically flawless, although it's almost painfully realistic. Mona Barrie, also starred, gives a convincing portrayal of an older woman who sincerely wishes to help the artist. (*Boxoffice*)

Hugo Haas quadruples in brass for *Strange Fascination* but might have done better by distributing the chores, especially in the script department. The story is overlong, overburdened, a little bit too pat in its resolutions and a little bit too ponderous in its conflict for popular fare. As an actor and producer, Haas fares much better. Producer Haas has a well-mounted show, dressed handsomely and set appropriately. Actor Haas develops a strong characterization as a concert pianist who is the victim of his middle-aged fancies, almost single-handedly elicits whatever sympathy and emotion the picture builds. Director Haas, however, unfolds his story slowly and awkwardly and is guilty of weak casting in supporting roles. Other than Haas' convincing portrayal, Mona Barrie, as the widow, is effectively warm and dignified as the situation requires. Cleo Moore, the dancer, is generally weak in a series of superficial poses and the others

CLEO, FRANK HILLIARD AND RICK VALLIN.

in the cast have little chance to register. Technical credits are adequate. (*Hollywood Reporter*)

Strange Fascination is another "one-man" production from Hugo Haas. For he wrote, directed, produced and stars in this Columbia release as in his previous *The Girl on the Bridge* and *Pickup*. Latest Haasian entry has a sordid, sexy theme in keeping with his earlier efforts. As such it rates as a fine subject for exploitation houses but appears to have a spotty feature in general release. Despite some good performances, the cast doesn't quite make the script believable. Haas' portrayal of the concert artist is in the sympathetic vein. Miss Moore easily fulfils the physical demands of her role but falls short of meeting the thespian requirements. Miss Barrie, as the sponsor, carries on with a platonic spirit one would expect a wealthy socialite to have. Rick Vallin, Karen Sharpe and Marc Krah, among others, provide fair support in lesser roles. (*Variety*)

Haas, who performs the four-way duty of producer, writer, director and star, carefully fashions the dramatic aspects of the plot and weaves a fine concert background into the footage. In each of his employments his work is outstanding. An attractive looker, Miss Moore scores brightly in

CLEO AND HUGO HAAS.

a somewhat difficult role, and she's bound to go places as a result of her performance. Mona Barrie, in part of Haas' sponsor, endows character with sympathetic understanding. Standout bits are contributed by Rick Vallin, Karen Sharpe, Genevieve Aumont and Marc Krah. Balance of the technical credits are of high standard, including Rudi Feld's art direction, Merrill G. White's editing and Paul Ivano's lensing. (*Variety Daily*)

The best that can be said for *Strange Fascination* is that it is a sincere treatment of a heavy-handed story lacking in surprises or originality. Hugo Haas, who wrote, produced, directed and acted in the drama, has provided a character study of unrelieved dreariness. Haas offers an excellent portrayal of the tortured musician. Cleo Moore, as the ambitious girl, is attractive but not too seasoned an actress. Mona Barrie gives conviction to the role of the sponsor. (*Buffalo Courier-Express*)

NOTES: Texas born Karen Sharpe (1934) had one of her first movie parts in this movie. She played in B-movies mostly. TV gave Karen starring parts in several iconic TV shows. She was married to producer and director Stanley Kramer from 1966 till his death in 2001. About working with Hugo Haas, Karen remarked: "I thought the film was a good little film. I saw it not so long ago and I thought that Hugo was a very big talent. I wish he could have been more of a success because I think he deserved to be. I think he was that talented. I was a little afraid of him because I heard he was a real tyrant. But actually, I never saw that in him either, he was very kind and very sweet to me."[24]

Strange Fascination was one of the last movie appearances of actress Mona Barrie (1909-1964). Born in London, United Kingdom, she was raised in Australia. She was known as a second-rate Kay Francis in the 1930s. Cleo's co-star Rick Vallin (1919-1977) was born in Russia and starred in B-movies in the 1940s and 1950s. He had the privilege to star with pre-fame Ava Gardner in *Ghosts on the Loose* (1943). French actress Geneviève Aumont (1924-1989) changed her professional name to Michele Montau.

Hugo's portrayal of Paul Marvan was an homage to his brother, concert pianist Pavel Haas, who was murdered in Auschwitz in October 1944. Milan Hain, author of an article called *Hugo Haas — Forgotten Émigré*, writes: "His death — combined with the tragic fate of Haas' father

24. Source: telephone conversation with author.

Zikmund, who died a few months earlier in Terezín — had a profound effect on Haas, who loved his family above everything else. Pavel's photograph can be seen in several scenes. Hugo Haas often furnished sets with objects of sentimental value — not so much for the audience to spot them but for himself, to make his films even more personal."[25]

Filming started on March 19, 1952. The movie was released in September 1952.

The National Legion of Decency rated the movie in category B, objecting, "Reflects the acceptability of divorce."

CLEO AND GENEVIÈVE AUMONT.

25. *Noir City.* Winter 2012

"I confess
I'm the kind of
girl every
man wants
but shouldn
marry!"
COLUMBIA PICTURES
presents
One Girl's
Confession
STARRING
CLEO MOORE · HUGO HAAS · GLENN
Written, Produced and Directed by HUGO HAAS

ONE GIRL'S CONFESSION

1953 — Columbia Pictures
74 minutes — Black and White

DIRECTOR: Hugo Haas. PRODUCER: Hugo Haas and Robert Erlik. SCENARIO: Hugo Haas. PHOTOGRAPHY: Paul Ivano. MUSIC: Vaclav Divina. EDITING: Merrill G. White. MAKEUP: Gustaf Norin. SOUND: Ben Winkler. SCRIPT SUPERVISOR: Joe Franklin. DIALOGUE SUPERVISOR: Mark Lowell.

CAST: **Cleo Moore** *(Mary Adams)*; Hugo Haas *(Dragomie Damitrof)*; Glenn Langan *(Johnny)*; Ellen Stansbury *(Judy)*; Anthony Jochim *(Father Benedict)*; Burt Mustin *(Gardener)*; Leonid Snegoff *(Old Gregory)*; Jim Nusser *(Warden)*; Russ Conway *(Police Officer)*; Mara Lea *(Girl)*; Gayne Whitman *(District Attorney)*; Leo Mastovoy *(Gambler)*; Martha Wentworth *(Old Lady)*; Arthur Marshall *(Bartender)*; Jan Englund *(Inmate)*; Sidney Fallender *(Bit part)*.

STORY: Mary Adams is employed in a tawdry waterfront restaurant owned by Old Gregory, who makes her life miserable. Years previously, he had robbed Mary's father of his fortune, and she plots to get even with him. When Gregory makes an illegal deal with a stranger and is paid $25,000, Mary steals the money and buries it in the woods. She admits the crime when the police question her but refuses to reveal the hiding place. Her good behaviour in prison shortens her sentence, but once free she bides her time before digging up the fortune. She obtains a job in a restaurant owned by Dragomie Damitrof, and strikes up a friendship with Johnny, a young fisherman. Damitrof, an inveterate gambler, loses everything one night, and Mary offers to help him cover his losses. She instructs him how to find the money she buried, but finding nothing, he returns and reviles her for tricking him. While brooding over the disappearance of the money, Mary learns that Damitrof is living in luxury in a penthouse, and she concludes that he is doing it with her money. She forces her way into the apartment while he is sleeping off a "drunk," and demands her money. A struggle follows, and she hits him over the head with a champagne bottle. Believing him to be dead, she is frantic. Just then Judy, his girlfriend, arrives on the scene and informs Mary that Damitrof had won considerable money at cards. Mary rushes to the spot where she had buried the money and finds it. Remorseful, she passes the money through the iron grillwork of a church gate, then goes to the police to confess the killing. The police check

Damitrof's apartment and find that he is very much alive. Mary rushes back to the church to recover her money, but she is too late. Later, Damitrof meets Mary and suggests that she join him now that he is wealthy, but she prefers to join Johnny for a life of respectability and happiness.

REVIEWS: Mediocre program fare. The story is not only ordinary and trite, but it sets a bad example, for the heroine is shown robbing her employer on the pretext that he once cheated her father of his money. Another flaw shows the heroine shoving the stolen money under a church gate after she believes that she had killed her boss, but attempting to recover the money after learning he is still alive. In other words, the writer believed that his heroine could atone for her sin as long as she offered the stolen money to the church. This is indeed peculiar morality. It is apparent that Hugo Haas, the author-producer-director, as well as actor, realized that he had no story to speak of, for he has seen to it that Cleo Moore, the heroine, appears throughout in clothes that emphasizes her buxomness. There is hardly any comic relief. (*Harrison's Reports*)

A pretty girl and her stolen money are the story bait of *One Girl's Confession*, which Hugo Haas wrote, produced and directed, and in which he plays

the leading role very expertly. Luscious Cleo Moore plays the girl fairly well but misses out on some high dramatic moments; Glenn Langan is pleasant as the boyfriend, Ellen Stansbury fills the adventuress role nicely, and Burt Mustin does a character bit well. (*LA Times*)

Columbia has a contrived little potboiler in this latest Hugo Haas independent feature. It is a plodding programmer for fill-in bookings, using up 73 minutes of film to little avail. The title of *One Girl's Confession* has some minor exploitation possibilities, and plenty of lobby art can be lifted from the numerous profile shots of sweater clad, buxom Cleo Moore to go with title ballyhoo. Haas wrote, produced and directed, as well as holding down a co-star spot with Miss Moore and Glenn Langan. The hackneyed, uninspiring plot finds Miss Moore going through a lot of travail she brings on herself. Performances are about what might be expected from such a plot and Haas' direction is so measured it becomes pedestrian. Paul Ivano's photography mostly features well-angled shots of Miss Moore in tight knit goods. The music score is designed to fit the moody meller. (*Variety*)

One Girl's Confession is a rather tedious, old-fashioned type of drama that went out of style several decades ago. Produced, directed and written by Hugo Haas, who also stars, it is doubtful if this clumsily acted programmer

CLEO AND ARTHUR MARSHALL.

will stimulate much interest among audiences. Best thing about the production is the performance of Haas, a very fine actor who by sheer force of personality manages to inject a spark of vitality into what is otherwise drab film fare. On his other credits, however, Haas doesn't come off so well. His direction is too leisurely and too often the backgrounds are incongruous to the situation. Miss Moore needs a lot more work before she can carry successfully the weight of such a role such as offered here. Langan is engaging as her heart throb, although the part makes very little demand.

CLEO MOORE AND LEONID SNEGOFF.

Other performances are overdone to an obvious degree. Technical credits are merely adequate. (*Hollywood Reporter*)

NOTES: According to a *Hollywood Reporter* news items, Marc Snow, Francis Brandt, Mark Lowell, Hugh Murray, Pearl Early and Ernestine Barrier were cast, but their appearance in the film has not been confirmed.

Denver born Glenn Langan (1917-1991) had appeared on Broadway before he signed a movie contract at 20th Century-Fox in 1943. He was cast in *Hangover Square* (1945) and *A Bell for Adano* (1945), which also starred Hugo Haas. His popularity waned in the early 1950s and he turned to television. Today he is best remembered for the title part in *The Amazing Colossal Man* (1957).

Actress and singer Helene Stanton (1925-2017) was cast as Ellen Stansbury in *One Girl's Confession*, which also marks her film debut. In 1949 she became silent film actor Kenneth Harlan's eighth wife. The couple divorced in 1953. The Film Noir *The Big Combo* (1955) was her break-through role. Stanton turned blonde and appeared in several B-movies before leaving show business in 1957. In some way she was in competition with Cleo when she was under contract to Columbia Pictures in 1954. Her roles in *New Orleans Uncensored* (1955) and *Jungle Moon Men* (1955) could have easily been played by Cleo too.

One Girl's Confession was announced to start filming in November 1952 as *Blonde Poison* to be filmed at the Motion Picture Center. Other working titles of the film were *Story of a Bad Girl* and *Tough Girl*. The movie was released on April 6, 1953.

Although my personal favorite of Cleo's movies, *One Girl's Confession* is a confusing film to follow. The story has too many twists while the plot is very one-dimensional. Cleo's character is not the smartest, nor meanest, she has played in her seven movies with Haas. Mary Adams is an indecisive girl. Her plan to steal and keep her father's money is simple and not very well worked out. Mary does have her heart in the right place, but she would have been a more interesting character if she showed more of her

CLEO MOORE AND GLENN LANGAN

conniving character in this story about moral and love. Nevertheless, as said before, this is my favorite outing of the Haas-Moore team. Cleo is featured in every scene, dressed in typical tight-fitting outfits, wearing berets on her flaxen-haired coiffure. She has stunning close-ups throughout the film and looks even lovelier and sexier than she did in *Thy Neighbor's Wife* or *Strange Fascination*. The publicity material and artwork on the posters and lobby cards portray Cleo as a seductive, bad blonde. Taglines like, "I confess, I'm the kind of girl every man wants, but shouldn't marry" reinforce these images.

The National Legion of Decency rated the movie in category B, objecting, "Tends to condone taking the law into one's own hands; suggestive costuming and situations."

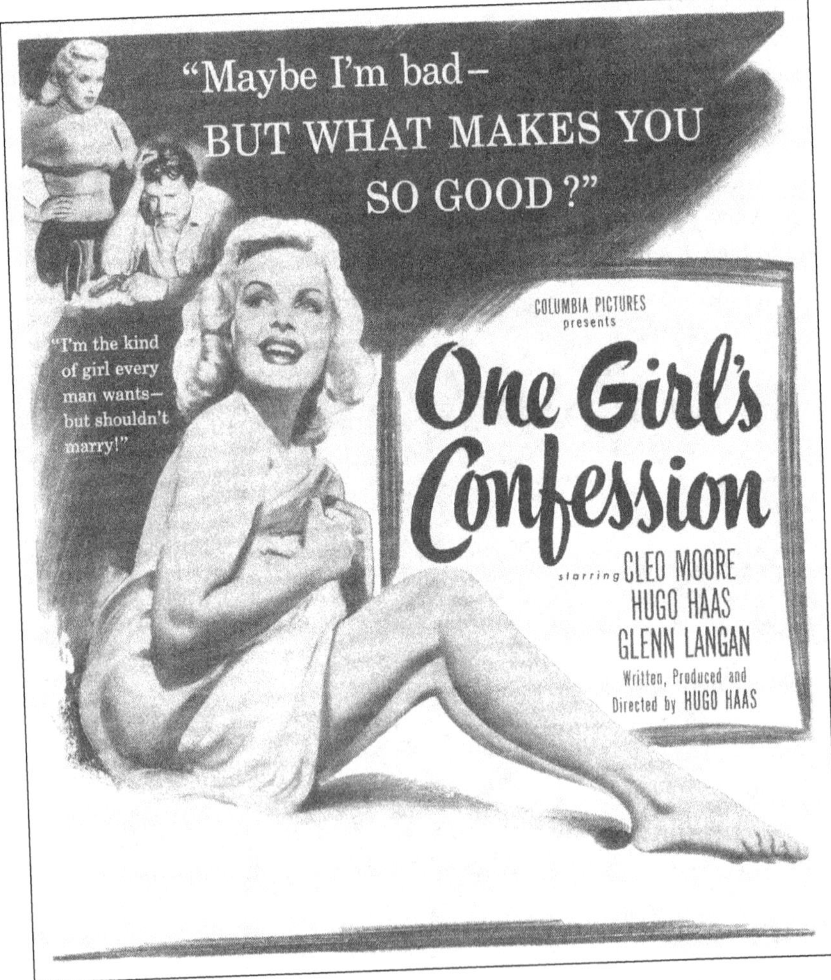

BAIT

1954 — Columbia Pictures
79 minutes — Black and White

DIRECTOR: Hugo Haas. PRODUCER: Hugo Haas and Robert Erlik.
SCENARIO: Samuel W. Taylor, based on his story. ADDITIONAL DIA-
LOGUE: Hugo Haas. PHOTOGRAPHY: Edward P. Fitzgerald. MUSIC:
Vaclav Divina. EDITING: Robert S. Eisen. SOUND: Benjamin Winkler.
SCRIPT SUPERVISOR: Wiliam E. Orr.

CAST: **Cleo Moore** *(Peggy);* Hugo Haas *(Marko);* John Agar *(Ray
Brighton);* Emmett Lynn *(Foley);* Bruno Ve Sota *(Webb);* Jan Englund
(Waitress); George Keymas *(Chuck);* Sir Cedric Hardwicke *(Satan in
Prologue).*

STORY: Marko, a Northern California prospector whose stories about a
lost gold mine had given him the reputation of a crackpot, makes a deal
with Ray Brighton, a young farmer, to search for the mine. Working fast
and hard to beat the winter snows in the mountain area, the two men

CLEO, HUGO HAAS AND JOHN AGAR.

succeed in finding the mine. The thought of giving up half the gold to Ray irks Marko, and he conceives the idea of marrying Peggy, a waitress with a shady reputation, who was in need of security and protection. Marko reasoned that, if he could tempt Ray to make love to Peggy, he could murder him under the "unwritten" law. Peggy accepts Marko's proposal of marriage and goes with him to the o-room mountain cabin where the three spend the winter, and where Marko watches his diabolic plot develop with satisfaction. Peggy and Ray do fall in love, but they do nothing wrong and give Marko no reason to suspect his wife's infidelity. In a final effort to force the issue, Marko pretends to go on a trip to town and leaves them alone in the cabin. But they discover his scheme and expose him. Taking Ray's share of the gold, the two young people leave Marko to start a new life for themselves, unaware that he had been left behind with a broken leg and would die of cold and hunger.

REVIEWS: This film is rather well acted, and sometimes skilfully directed by Haas, who also produced it. Miss Moore comes off best of all three. The usual action fan, however, will find it less interesting than the more mature theatregoer who often prefers dramatic dialogue to dramatic action. (*Hollywood Citizen News*)

Hugo Haas again weaves his story around a sex angle in his latest release, "Bait," a dramatic affair which, though well done, is somewhat more adult in treatment than general audiences prefer. Consequently, bookings will be to more selective situations. Yarn unfolds in a mountain cabin where three occupants, two men and a girl, are snowed in for the winter. Haas develops the situation with heavy dramatic overtones, and comes up with good performances all the way round. He injects the proper fanaticism into his own role, as he schemes to keep gold for himself; Miss Moore is both attractive and capable, and Agar strikes the right note in his enactment of a man in love with another's wife. Edward P. Fitzgerald's camera work lends a realistic note, and musical score by Vaclav Divina fits the mood. Other credits likewise are fitting. (*Variety*)

"Bait" is a film about gold fever, and other fevers which afflict humans, especially when a plumbing like Cleo Moore languishes between two men in a snowbound cabin. Haas' strong point in this film (as in the past) is his use of simple, effective settings and well-handled photography. (*LA Daily News*)

The picture falls somewhat short of its potentialities for exploring anew the theme of man's greed. Not that we expect Dostoievskian discourses, but the dialogue here is on a pretty primitive level. Even the Devil, who has had discussions with some interesting people in his time, sounds like a fledging demon reading the signposts along the path of evil. The performances on the other hand, are generally good. Miss Moore, to repeat, is capable, even though the camera is made to linger too long on her somatic assets. Haas, who also produced the picture, is a natural actor. Agar struck us as sophomoric at times, but was otherwise convincing. (*LA Examiner*)

Haas, who usually collaborates on the scripting, contributed additional dialog on this one. But more than extra conversation is needed to make the Taylor story ring with realism and plausibility. In what amounts to virtually a one-man affair. Haas makes good use of his limited production values, but his direction falls short of making the subject an absorbing one. His portrayal of the prospector is fair. Agar, acquits himself favourably as Haas' husky partner who for the most part restrains his instincts when femininity in the buxom shape of Miss Moore pervades the trio's one-room mountain cabin. She capably fills the moderate demands of

CLEO, HUGO HAAS AND JOHN AGAR.

her role and under some interesting camera angles shows that she can wear lingerie with the best of her contemporaries. (*Variety Daily*)

The picture is uneven, the dialogue undistinguished, and the machinations of the old prospector spelled out too completely because of the whisperings on sound track of devil Hardwicke for Haas. The introduction with Hardwicke in person, however, is effective and would have sufficed. The photography generally is well-angled and effective, catching at times the

CLEO AND JOHN AGAR.

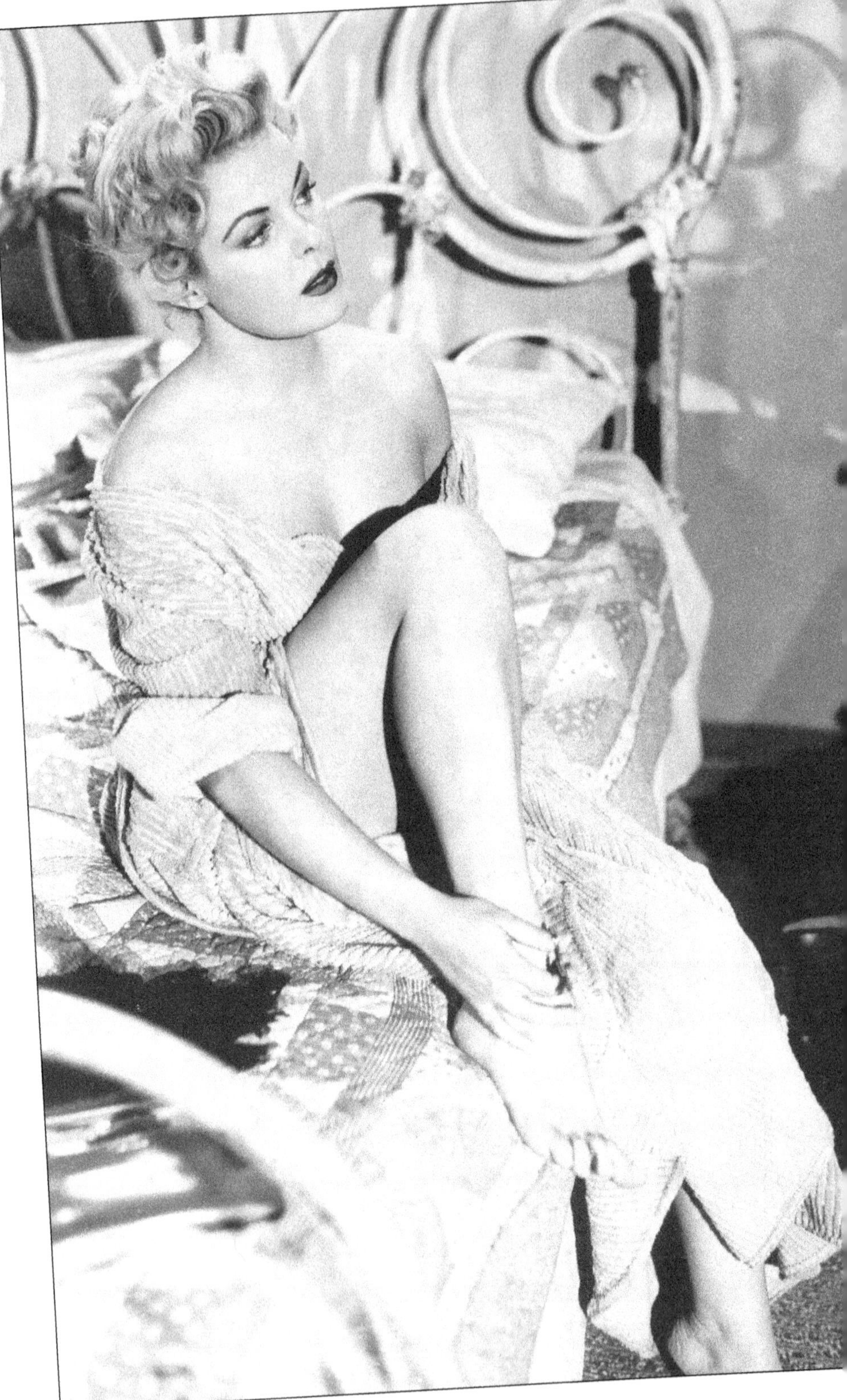

feeling the loneliness of the mountains. Miss Moore plays her role well. Agar, outside of the over-emotionalized gold-craze bit, is easy in character. Haas, without hindrance of the whisperings, is natural. (*Hollywood Reporter*)

Like the previous films produced by Hugo Haas, this one has been made on a modest budget with a story that places the accent on sex. As an entertainment it is only moderately interesting and somewhat unpleasant, but the subject matter has strong exploitation ingredients and for that reason should do well at the box-office as Haas' previous efforts.
Haas is acceptable in his role, as are Cleo Moore, as his buxom young wife, and John Agar, as his intended victim. A brief prologue in which Sir Cedric Hardwicke appears as the devil and sets the stage for Haas' wickedness adds nothing to the story. (*Harrison's Reports*)

The bait is blonde Cleo Moore and the man-trap is set for John Agar, in this oddly assorted melodrama. The other side of the triangle is provided by Hugo Haas, whose heavy-handed performance throws the flimsy story off balance. It's a log cabin melodrama heavily over-played. The most serious flaw is that the plot just doesn't hang together. The characters are blown up too large. Hugo Haas goes wide off the marks as the gold maniac; John Agar and Cleo Moore are unconvincing. (*Picturegoer*)

The brevity of the title of "Bait" at the Holiday is a fair indication of the brevity of everything else in this film. The short-change begins with the story, which is a pitifully meagre affair about how an old gold prospector brings a young wife to his cabin in the snow-bound hills in order to lure his young male partner into a situation where he may legally do him in. It is extended into the acting, which is leanly and laughingly done by Haas, who produced and directed, John Agar and Cleo Moore. And it is charitably completed by the comparative brevity of the film, which is the one shining virtue of it. We return the favor with this review. (*New York Times*)

NOTES: The marriage of Cleo and Haas is an arranged union. Haas uses her to set a trap for his partner Agar. Cleo, "Since our marriage ceremony you've never kissed me. You've never embraced me. And you let me sleep up there on the upper bunk. A woman, I mean a wife wants to belong. For her protection she wants to belong to her man, it gives her security. Don't you understand me? Now look at me. Don't I appeal to you?" Haas declines her invitation to consummate the marriage. That's the moment Cleo decides to start her affair with Agar. In a sexy bathtub scene she tries to seduce Haas, but also to seduce Agar. The haircut scene ignites the fire between Cleo and Agar. Agar says he is crazy about her and Cleo tries to fight her feelings. In the scene Cleo is using a pair of scissors, but no hair is cut.

The sexual tension is worked up with every scene in the film, until all this tension must come to a climax. About one of the bedroom scenes,

CENSORED BATHTUB PHOTO.

the *New York Post* columnist Sidney Skolsky mentions that "Cleo Moore, an overabundant blond, looks plenty sexy in a night shirt. The players run through the scene. Agar moves just close enough to Cleo to make it interesting for all concerned, and Cleo responds just enough to please the audience and satisfy the Johnson Office, Haas, trying to remain indifferent, speaks and acts excitedly. The scene is completed when actor Haas signals to the camera man, and then steps out to become director Haas. "You were fine, Cleo," says director Haas, "and you, John, performed exactly as I

told you. But I wasn't satisfied with that other actor's performance. Don't ham it up so much, Hugo!" Haas says in conclusion. "It isn't my acting," Hugo says to director Haas. "It's those lines! How can anyone read them without getting, shall I say, a little dramatic?" Cleo and Agar look toward the author. He appears puzzled. "I don't know about that," answers director Haas to actor Haas, "but I'll speak to writer Hugo Haas about it. One of me might be right."[26]

In the early fifties, John Agar (1921-2002) had gotten in trouble due to his alcoholism. He was thought to be unreliable, showing up on the set drunk. Hugo Haas and Agar made an unusual arrangement. "Kind of unusual arrangement for John Agar when he agreed to having a watchdog around during the filming of *Bait*, the new Hugo Haas picture. John has a penchant for trouble and on account of Haas took a chance on him; he was willing to have a fellow follow him around to see that he didn't give in to an unexpected impulse before he finished the picture. Everybody is pulling for Jack's success."[27]

Bait was filmed in the summer of 1953 under the working title *Fever*. The movie was released on February 24, 1954.

The National Legion of Decency rated the movie in category B, objecting, "Suggestive costuming, dialogue and situations."

THE OTHER WOMAN
1954 — 20th Century Fox
81 minutes — Black and White

DIRECTOR: Hugo Haas. PRODUCER: Hugo Haas and Robert Erlik. SCENARIO: Hugo Haas. PHOTOGRAPHY: Edward P. Fitzgerald. MUSIC: Ernest Gold. EDITING: Robert S. Eisen. MAKEUP: Morrie Hoffman. SOUND: Earl Snyder. SCRIPT SUPERVISOR: Gloria Alexander.

CAST: Hugo Haas *(Walter Darman)*; **Cleo Moore** *(Sherry Steward)*; Lance Fuller *(Ronnie)*; Lucille Barkley *(Mrs. Lucille Darman)*; Jack Macy *(Charles Lester)*; John Qualen *(Papasha)*; Jan Arvan *(Police Inspector Collins)*; Karolee Kelly *(Marion, Darman;s secretary)*; Steve Mitchell *(First Assistant Director)*; Mark Lowell *(Second Assistant Director)*; Melinda

26. *New York Post*, June 25, 1953.

27. *Screenland plus TV-Land*, September 1953.

Markey *(Script girl);* Anthony Jochim *(Pathologist);* Jan Englund *(Jan, bit player);* Arthur Marshall *(bit part);* Sue Casey *(bit part);* Sharon Dexter *(bit part);* Ivan Haas *(newspaper boy).*

STORY: Walter Darman, director of a Hollywood production, asks Sherry Steward, a bit player, to read several lines of dialogue. Dissatisfied, he rejects her for a small part in the picture and she vows to get even with him. Together with Ronnie, her boyfriend, she devises an ingenious way to lure Darman to her apartment, where she drugs his drink and renders him unconscious. As a result of this incident, she leads Darman to believe that she's pregnant and demands $50,000 from him lest she create a scandal. This predicament causes him so much worry that Lucille, his wife, senses that something is wrong. It also leads to a violent argument with Charles Lester, his father-in-law, head of the producing company. When Sherry threatens to go to his wife unless payment is forthcoming immediately, Darman, after carefully establishing an alibi for himself, secretly goes to her apartment and strangles her to death. The crime, through circumstantial evidence, is blamed on Papasha, a peddler, but in the end Darman's conscience gets the better of him and he gives himself up to the police.

CLEO AND MARK LOWELL.

REVIEWS: Like most of the other pictures produced independently by Hugo Haas, this one is notable for the lurid overtones of the story, but it shapes up as a fair program melodrama that is best suited for adult audiences. The screenplay, which revolves around a scheming, vindictive film extra who compromises a Hollywood director in an effort to blackmail him, serves up a mixture of sex, violence and murder that is far from pleasant, but it gives the voluptuous Cleo Moore ample opportunity to make the most of her physical attributes. Her characterization, however, is unbelievable. Haas turns in his usual good performance as the victimized

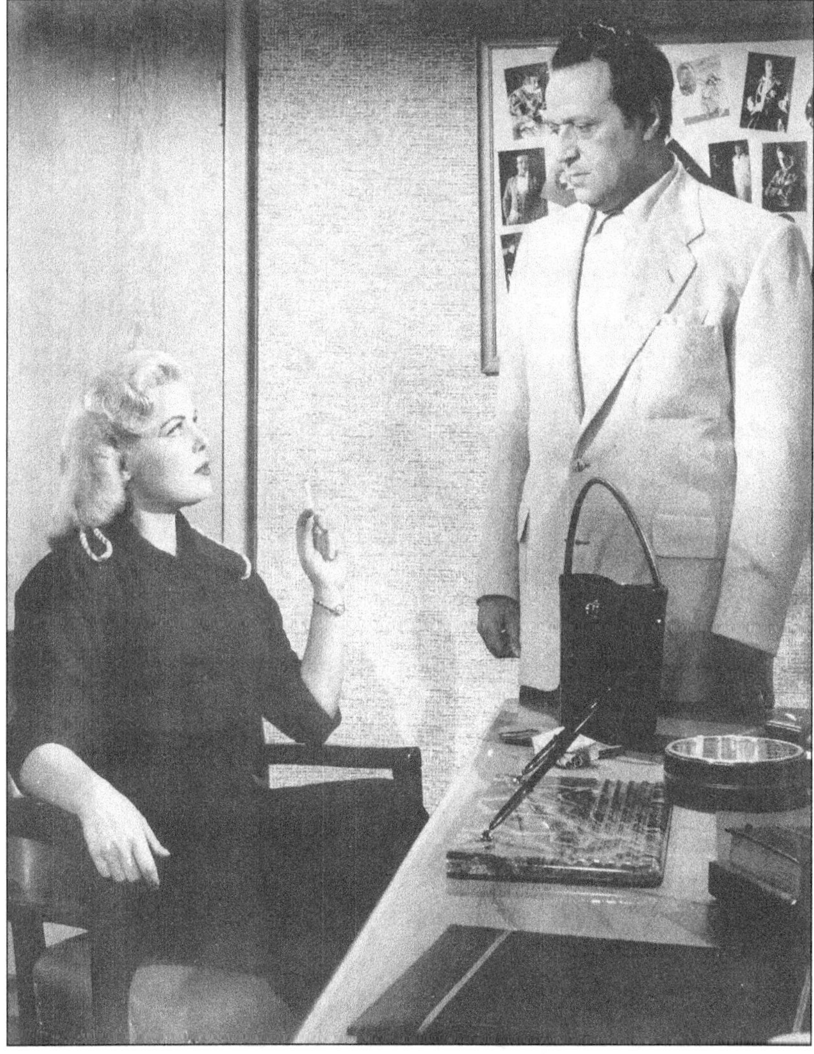

CLEO AND HUGO HAAS.

director. The story's film industry background and atmosphere should prove interesting to the picture-goers. (*Harrison's Reports*)

Hugo Haas plays a famous Continental director who, having turned down a small-part actress for lack of talent, is faced with her plot to ruin him. Cleo Moore plays the girl as revengeful and vixenish a blackmailer as could be. (*Picturegoer*)

This is just another movie. Laid in Hollywood, it explains how movie directors must be constantly on guard to protect their honor from girl bit players. (*Hollywood Reporter*)

"*The Other Woman*" suggests that Haas, perhaps should not try to star, write and direct but delegate some of these tasks to others, since this might have been much better if he had not tried to do it all by himself. However, pic should make money because like Haas' predecessors it does not look to be an expensive effort and has enough sex and drama to attract in lesser situations. Haas is standout as the foreign director-producer. He derives a better story. Miss Moore, a curvaceous looker, is good as the unsuccessful but scheming extra. Lucille Barkley as Haas' wife, is excellent and has enough promise to justify bigger roles. Lance Fuller, as Miss Moore's boyfriend, does well enough in the part of a teenage gangster. John Qualen is submerged in a lesser role, but handles it in his usual capable manner. Haas' directing is far ahead of his scripting, while his production job is up to his standard. Robert S. Eisen has edited skilfully and the lensing of Eddie Fitzgerald is outstanding. (*Variety*)

"*The Other Woman*" is a typical Hugo Haas production. There are times when the dialogue is loaded with realism and other's when it's just ludicrous. The character of the director is conceived logically while that of the girl is completely lacking in motivation or other than a bare hint or two that she might be unbalanced. However, it always manages to hold the

CLEO MOORE AND LANCE FULLER.

interest and should be fairly well received by adult audiences. The acting is generally good although Miss Moore's version of sex-appeal is too stilted. The supporting cast is unknown. (*Motion Picture Daily*)

NOTES: A movie within a movie. Hollywood's Hollywood. Cleo is an extra playing cards on the set where Haas is the director. When a bit player is unable to attend, he asks Cleo to take her place. She calls her boyfriend to tell him she got a part with three speaking lines. When he doesn't react enthusiastically, we see the hard side of Cleo. She blows her chance and Hugo and the rest of the cast ridicule her. When she gets home, she finds her boyfriend, Lance Fuller, playing cards with friends. She sends the guys away and brushes off Lance. When she is calmed down, she tells what happened and swears she will take revenge. Lance thinks she's hysterical when she tells him her idea of blackmailing Haas. Nevertheless, he helps her with her plans to ruin the director. In one scene, Cleo looks stunning in a glittering strapless evening dress and white fur when she attends the wrap party for Haas' movie. She dances with him and at the end of the evening makes sure he will bring her home. Again, we witness the scheming side of her character when she drugs Haas as part of her blackmail plan. When she makes her demands, $50,000, Hugo tells her she is crazy. "What did you expect? That you could pay my fare back to Louisiana?" Cleo snaps. Cleo and her character Sherry blended into one with this one sentence in the dialogue. Although not all of Cleo's dialogue is convincing, she makes the most of a sketchy part and plays the scheming, bad blonde with a hint of psychological imbalances, quite effectively. Where Mary Adams of *One Girl's Confession* took off, Sherry Steward picks up the scheming, plotting, and blackmailing. She is the typical film noir bad girl, out to ruin a man until there is nothing left of him but broken pieces. Of course, that amount of evilness and selfish behavior had to be punished in the 1950's. A girl like Sherry couldn't set an example of how women should behave. She, just like the adulteress in *Thy Neighbor's Wife*, has to be punished and pay her wicked ways with the highest price, her life.

"*The Other Woman* is Haas' most ambitious film, with many themes and motives mirroring his own career: life in exile characterized by disillusionment and entrapment, loss of one's identity and social status, hopeless struggle with the Hollywood machinery, and the impossibility of fully realizing one's artistic visions."[28]

28. Milan Hain. *Hugo Haas — Forgotten Émigré.* Noir City, winter 2012.

Co-star Lance Fuller (1928-2001) recalled about working with Hugo Haas, "The movie was originally called *Turmoil* but ended up as *The Other Woman,* and it was a crime melodrama, a revenge plot. I was a very close friend of Hugo Haas. He directed me every way. I remember his direction. I kind of got lost in the part. I was having a bit of a problem, and he pulled me out of it. He was an excellent director and an excellent filmmaker. I remember him writing scripts and doing everything himself. He was a one-man show like Orson Welles. Hugo Haas and Cleo Moore were nice people too." Fuller was a bit player when he met starlet Joi Lansing on the set of *The Merry Widow* (1952) at MGM. They were married between 1951 and 1953. Universal-International took him under contract where he made his debut in Mamie Van Doren's *All American* (1953). Fuller also appeared in several cult classics: *This Island Earth* (1955), *The She-Creature* (1956), *Voodoo Woman (1957)* and *The Bride and the Beast* (1958).

Melinda Markey (1934), daughter of actress Joan Bennett, appeared in the scene were Cleo keeps forgetting her lines. "Hugo Haas was always a gentleman to me. There was never a problem, never an issue, everything was fine." Unfortunately, Melinda doesn't remember Cleo, "I get a picture, but I don't remember any specifics about her. I remember her face, but nothing specific." Melinda worked pleasantly with Cleo and all other crew

CLEO AND HUGO HAAS.

and cast members. "I was very fortunate in my career. I got along with everybody."[29]

The Other Woman marked the screen debut of stage and television actor Jack Macy. Former Conover model Lucille Barkley (1924-1979) got some nice reviews but wasn't handed any good material after *The Other Woman*. Her last movie was *Women's Prison*, cast as an inmate with Cleo. Hugo's secretary is played by Karolee Kelly aka Carol Kelly (1931-2017). She's a statuesque blonde looker, a cross between Cleo and Beverly Michaels.

The Other Woman was filmed in the first two weeks of April and was released on December 2, 1954.

The National Legion of Decency rated the movie in category B, objecting, "Suggestive costuming, dialogue and situations."

HOLD BACK TOMORROW

1955 — Universal-International
75 minutes — Black and White

DIRECTOR: Hugo Haas. PRODUCER: Hugo Haas and Robert Erlik. SCENARIO: Hugo Haas. PHOTOGRAPHY: Paul Ivano. MUSIC: Sidney B. Cutner. EDITING: Henry De Mond. WARDROBE: Morrie Friedman. SOUND: Earl Snyder.

CAST: John Agar *(Joe Cardos)*; **Cleo Moore** *(Dora)*; Frank DeKova *(Priest)*; Dallas Boyd *(Warden)*; Steffi Sidney *(Clara Cardos)*; Mel Welles *(First Guard)*; Harry Guardino *(Detective)*; Mona Knox *(Escort girl)*; Arlene Harris *(Madame)*; Kay Riehl *(Warden's wife)*; Jan Englund *(Girl)*; Pat Goldin *(Dancing Comedian)*.

STORY: Awaiting execution in a death cell, Joe Cardos, a convicted killer, is so bitter that he even refuses to see his sister Clara. The prison warden informs Joe that he will be supplied with anything he wants, as is customary on the last night on earth for those who are to be executed. At first, Joe refuses anything and everything, but he relents at the last minute and requests that he be supplied with a woman. The warden is shocked by the request, but he decides to fulfil it in the belief that he has no way out. He sends two of his representatives out to find a woman who would be willing to spend the night with Joe, and they come across Dora, a despondent girl,

29. Source: telephone conversation with author, 12-08-2015.

who had just been dragged out of the sea after an attempt to drown herself. She accepts the proposition that is made to her and is taken to Joe's cell. The two talk all through the night and, as dawn approaches, they find that he had fallen in love with each other. Before he is led to the gallows, Joe asks that he and Dora be married. The priest complies with the request after much hesitation. The closing scene finds Joe heading for the gallows while Dora and Clara pray for a miracle.

REVIEWS: The consciences of those in the Johnston office who have charge of approving stories and granting production code seals must have taken innumerable tumbles and somersaults to induce them to pass this story. It deals with a convicted man who, on the eve of his execution, is granted a last request — a woman to comfort and amuse him in his final hours. Although the warden conveniently supplies him with a woman, nothing, of course, happens physically, but the very thought of the request should prove repulsive to most of those who will see it. To say that the acting is good cannot excuse the team, which is best suited for those theatres that specialize in sensational exploitation methods. Most of the action centers on the dialogue between the convict and the girl. The photography is just as somber at the theme. (*Harrison's Reports*)

U-I has picked up a good second-half of the bill in Hugo Haas' "Hold Back Tomorrow." The film is a small budgeter that is perfect for the "leather jacket crowd." It has enough sex to arouse comment and can figure on a healthy share of exploitation value from its offbeat story. Haas had a good idea in his screenplay — a condemned prisoner being allowed his request to spend his last night with a beautiful woman — but the development of his theme was weak. However, he has maintained a moody European flavor in his film that serves it well and, except for a slack story middle, he has done an adequate job as writer-director-producer. Both Miss Moore

and Agar work hard and turn in competent performances. Paul Ivano turns in an effective camera job. The title song by lyricist Franz Steininger and Johnny Rotella, while not of hit proportions, integrates the film nicely. (*Hollywood Reporter*)

As usual with the independent pix turned out by Hugo Haas, this one tackles a subject not likely to be tried by larger companies. Results are fairly okay, but other than the exploitation angle it's a program entry. Picture, which Haas wrote, produced and directed, and which Universal is releasing,

centers virtually all of the action on Miss Moore and Agar. Sometimes they get in over their dramatic depth, but generally acquit themselves quite well in enacting the offbeat plot. Frank de Kova is good as a priest, and among others more prominently involved are Dallas Boyd, the warden; Steffi Sidney, the killer's young sister, and Mel Welles, a guard. *(Variety Daily)*

Written, produced and directed by Hugo Haas, this Universal release will have to lean heavily on the exhibitor's showmanship to realize any worthwhile returns. The production is "quickie" all the way, and neither John Agar nor Cleo Moore add to their laurels with the performances they turn in. Haas was apparently experimenting with a "naturalistic" mood and projection of character (which has "touches" like Miss Moore belching after eating a highly-seasoned cabbage soup and Agar telling a prison guard that he has to go to the men's room) and this off-beat tone might intrigue some. The direction is well-enough paced. (*Film Bulletin*)

Hugo Haas has again attacked a story premise that is daring and offbeat and has come up with an exploitable and well-done motion picture.

CLEO AND JOHN AGAR.

This time he deals with the last request of a young strangler, sentenced to hang for murder, in an international port. The strangler's last request is a woman's companionship on his last night. A fine script and careful direction gives the film smoothness and depth that are worthy of a much bigger budget. Cleo Moore and John Agar deliver excellent performances. (*The Independent Film Journal*)

Here's a movie made to order for New Year's Day, when your vision is groggy, your senses dull, and your judgement pretty tolerant. The theme is completely unpreachy, and the plot is simplicity itself. It's sure to provide a slew of unintentional laughs. (*Screen Stories*)

Here's a real happy movie. Starts with Cleo Moore diving in a river and cursing the guy who yanks her out. But she was saved for a higher purpose, to cast some form of ecstasy into the remaining hours of girl-killer (he strangles 'em) John Agar's life. Cleo, or for that matter any girl, is his last request and the warden can't find it in him to refuse. Well, it all goes to show you never know how or where you're going to meet Mr. Right. Cleo's joy, I'm sorry to say, is necessarily short-lived. (*Modern Screen*)

NOTES: Purchased outright for release by Universal-International. The original version of the independently made picture ran into some trouble with the Production Code Authority because of the treatment of the content of the story. The screenplay was sent to the PCA office for approval in September 1954. It was found to be utterly unacceptable as it portrayed illicit sex and had "no voice for morality or compensating moral values."

Essentially a two-character play, Haas added some scenes, but most of the action takes place in Agar's prison cell. This is the only movie where Hugo Haas wasn't starred with Cleo.

John Agar (1921-2002) had once been Shirley Temple's husband. After a promising start of his career in the 1940s, he was considered difficult to deal with, because of his alcoholism. He appeared in many B-movies that are considered cult classics these days. Some titles: *Revenge of the Creature* (1955), *Tarantula* (1955), *The Mole People* (1956), *The Brain from Planet Arous* (1957) and *Attack of the Puppet People* (1958).

In January 1955 *Hold Back Tomorrow* is being edited and scored. Haas shot the film at the Kling Studios, formerly known as Charlie Chaplin studios. In October 1955 Universal Studios released the picture.

"Refusal of the PCA to grant the screenplay a tentative Seal of Approval did not, however, prevent Haas from making the film. In February 1955, he sent a copy of the finished picture to Joseph Breen only to receive another, perhaps even stricter *no*. What followed were months of deletions and changes until, finally, in July 1955, *Hold Back Tomorrow* was approved."[30]

The National Legion of Decency rated the movie in category A-II and held no objection.

WOMEN'S PRISON

1955 — Columbia Pictures
80 minutes — Black and White

DIRECTOR: Lewis Seiler. PRODUCER: Bryan Foy. SCENARIO: Crane Wilbur and Jack DeWitt, based on an original story by Jack DeWitt. PHOTOGRAPHY: Lester H. White. MUSIC: Mischa Bakaleinikoff. EDITING: Henry Batista. SET DECORATION: Louis Diage. ART DIRECTION: Cary Odell. SOUND: George Cooper.

CAST: Ida Lupino *(Amelia van Zandt)*; Jan Sterling *(Brenda Martin)*; **Cleo Moore** *(Mae)*; Audrey Totter *(Joan Burton)*; Phyllis Thaxter *(Helene Jensen)*; Howard Duff *(Dr. Crane)*; Warren Stevens *(Glen Burton)*; Barry Kelley *(Warden Brock)*; Gertrude Michael *(Chief Matron Sturgess)*; Vivian Marshall *(Dottie LaRose)*; Mae Clarke *(Matron Saunders)*; Ross Elliot *(Don Jensen)*; Adelle August *(Grace)*; Don C. Harvey *(Chief Guard Tierney)*; Juanita Moore *(Polyclinic 'Polly' Jones)*; Edna Holland *(Sarah Graham)*; Murray Alper *(Mae's Boyfriend)*; Jana Mason *(Josie)*; Lynn Millan *(Carol)*; Frances Morris *(Miss Whittier)*; Wanda Barbour, Lucille Barkley, June Benbow, Sue Carlton, Lucia Carroll, Marge Davies, Mary Lou Devore, Gay Fairchild, Vera Francis, Jeanne Gail, Julie Gehring, Marcoreta Hellman, Joyce Johnson, Beverly Kidd, Jarma Lewis, Kathy Marlowe, Mara McAfee, Laurie Mitchell, Geraldine Pattison, Lonnie Pierce, Phyllis Planchard, Angela Stevens, Merry Townsend, Ruth Vann, Dorothy Vernon, Ruth Whitney *(Inmates)*; Madge Cleveland, Jean Harvey, Beatrice Maude, Riza Royce, Dorothy Ryan *(Matrons)*; Jack Kenney, Mike Mahoney, Lee Martin, Tyler McVey *(Guards)*; Diane DeLaire *(Head Nurse)*; Eddie Foy III *(Warden's Trustee)*; Mary Newton *(Laundry Matron Enright)*; Frank O'Connor *(Convict)*; Frank Sully *(Frank; Turnkey)*; Lorna Thayer *(Deputy Sheriff Green)*; Steve Benton *(Bit Part)*.

30. Milan Hain. *Hugo Haas — Forgotten Émigré.* Noir City, winter 2012.

SENSATIONAL SCANDAL
ROCKS WOMEN'S PRISON!
"With money you can buy anything in here!"
29345
"Even behind bars, a smart gal can have a ball."
60781
REVEAL "LOVE NEST ALLEY"!
Women riot over sin expose!
"The fix was in, but the price got too high."
33706
starring
IDA LUPINO
JAN STERLING
CLEO MOORE
AUDREY TOTTER
PHYLLIS THAXTER
and
HOWARD DUFF
WOMEN'S PRISON
Play by CRANE WILBUR and JACK DeWITT • Produced by BRYAN FOY • Directed by LEWIS SEILER • A COLUMBIA PICTURE

STORY: Sentenced to prison because of an unfortunate automobile accident that had caused the death of a child, Helene Jensen, a housewife, is terrified by the new surroundings. The other women prisoners sympathize with her and resent the callous treatment accorded to her by Amelia Van Zandt, the power-loving supervisor, who resented the fact that her charges had escaped the man-less life she had lived. Despite Dr. Crane's warning that Helene was upset, Amelia's cruelties almost result in her near death from nervous shock, but Crane nurses her back to health with delicate skill. One day, Glen Burton, a convict in the men's section, manages to smuggle himself into the women's section for a meeting with his wife Joan, who had been sentenced with him in connection with a robbery. This meeting results in Joan becoming pregnant, and the situation alarms Warden Brock, who is unable to make Glen reveal how he got into the women's section. To save his own neck, Brock warns Amelia that she will lose her job unless she gets the information from Joan Burton. Ignoring Joan's pregnancy, Amelia puts her through a vicious third-degree grilling day and night and, in a fit of anger, beats her. This brings on a miscarriage and her eventual death. Infuriated, the women prisoners, led by Brenda Martin, stage a rebellion, over-power the matrons and capture Amelia. Meanwhile Glen Burton smuggles himself back into the section, determined to kill Amelia.

Before he can harm her, however, the guards, using tear gas, reestablish control. Amelia, terrified by the experience, becomes a raving maniac. The movie ends with Dr. Crane assuring the prisoners that immediate reforms will be instituted.

REVIEWS: Columbia has a highly exploitable, well made prison melodrama here. The picture's gimmick, a prison with women inmates on one side and men on the other with only stone walls between them, is a strong theme and is well developed. Another factor is the lineup of femme

toppers, all of whom mean something at the marquee: Ida Lupino, Jan Sterling, Cleo Moore, Audrey Totter and Phyllis Thaxter. Thrown in for good measure is Howard Duff, himself a potent ticket seller. The general overall top performing of all these players gives the film a tautness and a sense of the melodramatic, which make its unreeling pass quickly. The literate screen play has no cliché and no plot flaws and hold the audience's interest all the way. (*The Independent Film Journal*)

A grim but effective program prison melodrama, well directed and acted. The cast names are impressive and should enhance its box-office value. Set in a prison that houses inmates of both sexes, and centering around a sadistic supervisor of the women's section who mistreats her charges until they revolt against her cruelty, the story, though depressing, grips one's interest from start to finish and holds one in suspense. Ida Lupino, as the cruel supervisor, turns is an outstanding performance. Equally effective, but in a sympathetic way, is Howard Duff as the patient prison doctor who tries to protect the convicts. Capable characterizations are provided by Jan Sterling, Audrey Totter, Cleo Moore and Phyllis Thaxter as the principal women prisoners. (*Harrison's Reports*)

Picture succeeds in being sensational, sometimes substituting large amount of violence for dramatic honesty — but effectively. Good pace, good performances give this life. (*Independent Exhibitors Film Bulletin*)

Lewis Seiler's direction has good pace and keeps the interest level high. Under his handling, players etch generally fine portrayals. Ida Lupino is especially good as the power-loving prison head, and Howard Duff thoroughly competent as the doctor. Others prominent within the walls are Phyllis Thaxter, very good as the terror-stricken housewife in on a manslaughter charge for accidentally killing a child through reckless driving; Jan Sterling, fine as the hardened gal who can't seem to stay outside the walls; Cleo Moore, okay as the irrepressible character from the wrong side of the tracks; and Audrey Totter, fine as a likeable femme introduced to crime by her husband, confined in another part of the prison. Remaining roles are all well played, with an especially notable stint turned in by Vivian Marshall, a former stripper inmate who pleases with imitations of Bette Davis, Tallulah Bankhead and even Ida Lupino. (*Variety Daily*)

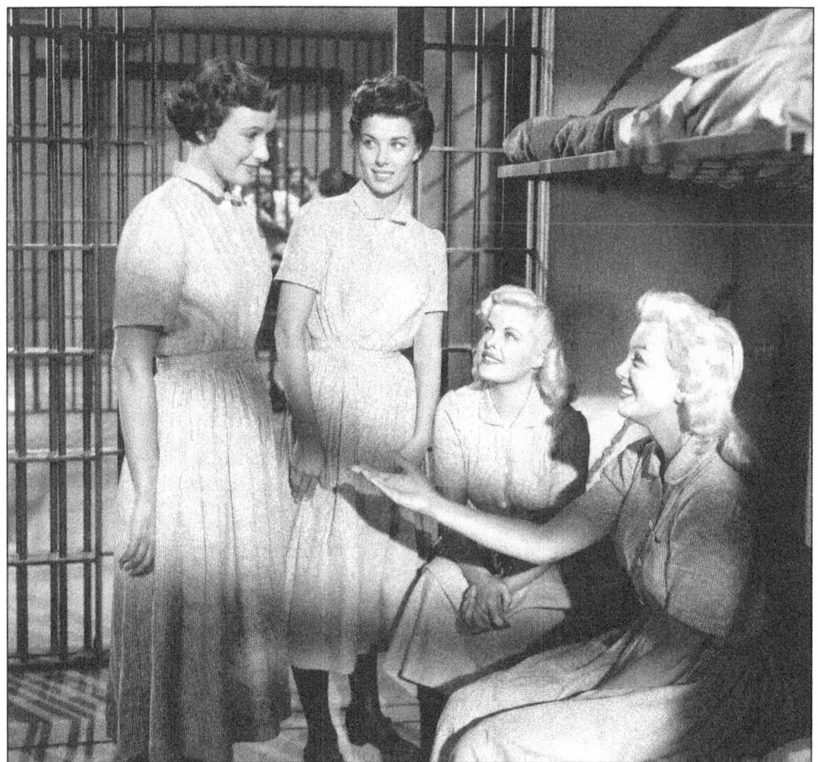

CLEO MOORE WITH PHYLLIS THAXTER, ADELLE AUGUST AND JAN STERLING.

There isn't much glamour in this story of ladies in the "Big House" but there are a number of strong characterizations and the melodrama provided by the script of Crane Wilbur and Jack DeWitt is professional and competent. Lewis Seiler's direction maintains pace and excitement, but it's hard to predict whether or not this title's subject matter will be box-office. In producing it, Bryan Foy made an intelligent gamble. Miss Lupino, Miss Sterling, and Miss Totter all give top performances. Cleo Moore and Vivian Marshall are good in comedy roles. Barry Kelley makes a convincing political hack out of the warden and Warren Stevens gets sympathy as the tense convict husband. Gertrude Michael makes a welcome reappearance on the screen as the head matron. But it still remains to be seen whether there is a hard-boiled audience for a hard-boiled picture about women. For the sake of all the talents involved, I hope that there is. (*Hollywood Reporter*)

Film is frequently depressing but good marquee values in the cast plus its exploitable subject will help this Bryan Foy production acquit itself favorably in the programmer market. Miss Lupino, in portraying the heavy, makes herself intensely disliked. Duff is an easy-going physician, patient

CLEO WITH MADGE CLEVELAND AND JAN STERLING.

and sympathetic despite his problems. Miss Sterling scores nicely as a tough moll, Cleo Moore is a typical femme inmate and Vivian Marshall, as an ex-stripteaser gone wrong, shines in some amusing impersonations. Phyllis Thaxter contribs a fine emotional study of a woman suffering from a guilt complex. (*Variety*)

In this slight switch on a familiar theme, Ida Lupino gives another of her forceful performances, this time as a sadistic lady warden. Howard Duff, Jan Sterling and Cleo Moore, among others, help out with satisfactory performances, but the general atmosphere is much too unpadded and intense for comfort. (*Newsweek*)

The roughest, toughest, rawest film about women ever made must be Columbia's *Women's Prison*, starring Ida Lupino, Jan Sterling, Cleo Moore, Audrey Totter, Phyllis Thaxter and one scared male, Howard Duff. It's the story of a prison in which the only barrier between man and women inmates is a wall which proves too weak. Scandal rocks the jail when a female prisoner proves to be pregnant. Ida Lupino, vicious warped, repressed superintendent in charge of the women's section, resents the fact that one of her

MADGE CLEVELAND, JAN STERLING, ADELLE AUGUST, GERTRUDE MICHAEL, CLEO AND PHYLLIS THAXTER.

inmates has escaped the man-less life that is hers. She cruelly beats up the culprit and that starts a riot. For sheer terrorism there is nothing quite like the stampede of female tigresses who go after Miss Lupino's blood. And for stark realism there is nothing quite like *Women's Prison*. (*Movie News*)

NOTES: Cleo has just a few scenes, some nice close-ups but for the most part she is lost in the group scenes. She plays a dumb blonde who's groomed by Sterling and the other inmates to talk like and become a lady. The other girls are teasing her and helping her to lose her hillbilly accent.

Laurie Mitchell (1928-2018) played a small part in the movie. "It almost appeared like we were in a real prison. It was on location. Being with Miss Ida Lupino, she was a firecracker. I mean rough, tough. It [being in a prison] made me feel kind of sad. God forbid, I would never want to be in this kind of situation. Jan Sterling was very nice to be with, very cooperative."[31]

Jan Sterling (1921-2001) played Cleo's pal in the movie. This talented blonde was married to actor Paul Douglas from 1950 to 1959, when he died from a heart attack. In the late 1960s she moved to England. Some of her other movies are: *Caged* (1950), *Ace in the Hole* (1951) with Kirk Douglas, *The High and the Mighty* (1954), *Female on the Beach* (1955) and *The Harder They Fall* (1956), with Humphrey Bogart.

The National Legion of Decency rated the movie in category B, objecting, "Suggestive sequences, tends to arouse disrespect for law and order."

OVER-EXPOSED

1956 — Columbia Pictures
80 minutes — Black and White

DIRECTOR: Lewis Seiler. PRODUCER: Lewis J. Rachmil. SCENARIO: James Gunn and Gil Orlovitz, based on an original story by Mary Loos and Richard Sale. PHOTOGRAPHY: Henry Freulich. MUSIC: Mischa Bakaleinikoff. EDITING: Edwin Bryant. MAKEUP: Clay Campbell. HAIR: Helen Hunt. COSTUME DESIGN: Jean Louis. SET DECORATION: Robert Priestley. ART DIRECTION: Carl Anderson. SOUND: Josh Westmoreland.

CAST: **Cleo Moore** *(Lila Crane)*; Richard Crenna *(Russell Bassett)*; Isobel Elsom *(Mrs. Payton Grange)*; Raymond Greenleaf *(Max West)*; Constance Towers *(Shirley Thomas)*; James O'Rear *(Roy Carver)*; Donald

31. Source: telephone conversation with author, 10-29-2017.

CLEO WITH
RICHARD CRENNA.

Randolph *(Coco Fields)*; Dayton Lummis *(Horace Sutherland)*; Jeanne Cooper *(Renee)*; Jack Albertson *(Les Bauer)*; Edna Holland *(Mrs. Gulick)*; Dick Crockett *(Jerry)*; Eddie Parker *(Matt)*; Geraldine Hall *(Martha)*; Voltaire Perkins *(Judge Evans)*; Joan Miller *(Fran)*; Helen Eby-Rock *(Mrs Grannigan)*; Frank Mitchell *(Steve, bartender)*; Norma Brooks *(Doris)*; Robert B. Williams *(Police Sergeant)*; Leon Alton, Cosmo Sardo Jeffrey Sayre, Franklyn Farnum, Dick Gordon, Philo McCullough, Bert Stevens *(Nightclub Patrons)*; Barbara Aler, Shirlee Allard *(Nightclub Girls)*; Robert Bice *(Patrolman)*; Barry Brooks *(Henchman)*; Chuck Cason *(Taxi Driver)*; John Cason *(Studio Thug)*; George Cisar *(Club Customer)*; Charles J. Conrad *(Policeman)*; Diane DeLaire *(Hysterical Woman)*; Bob Hopkins *(Operator)*; Lenore Kingston *(Nightclub Woman)*; Bill McLean *(Freddy, bellhop)*; Leo Mostovoy *(Mario, Maitre D' Club Coco)*; Roger Smith *(Reporter)*; Rudy Germane *(Gangster)*.

STORY: Down on her luck and living a sordid existence as a B-Girl in clip joints, Lila is befriended by Max West, a once famous photographer turned alcoholic, who teaches her how to handle a camera. With her new-found knowledge, Lila decides to try her luck in New York but

CLEO AND RAYMOND GREENLEAF.

to no avail. She meets and becomes friends with news reporter Russell Bassett, who helps her obtain a job as a camera girl in a second-rate night club. Once there, Lila uses her wiles on the manager and succeeds in ousting another girl photographer, thus gaining the whole concession for herself. She grabs an opportunity to better herself by snapping a compromising photograph of Horace Sutherland. He's a lawyer for a notorious gangster. Lila then uses the picture as a mild form of blackmail to persuade Sutherland to give her the photographer's job in an exclusive night club owned by his gangster boss. There she snaps and cleverly

CLEO AND RICHARD CRENNA.

doctors a photograph of Mrs. Payton, an aged society dowager, who is so pleased by the flattering picture that it establishes Lila as a leading society figure. She wins fame and fortune and sends for Max to be her assistant. One night she manages to snap Mrs. Payton as she dies from a heart attack while dancing at the club. Lila, out of respect for the old lady, does not release the photograph, but it is stolen from her file by an unscrupulous gossip columnist, who publishes it. Believing that she had sold the photo, all her newfound society friends turn against her and she goes broke. Now desperate, Lila uses an incriminating photo that could land the gangster in jail in an attempt to blackmail him into buying it.

The gangster dispatches several thugs to beat up Lila and obtain the photo. Russell, learning that she is in trouble, manages to rescue her. After informing the police of what she knows about the gangster, Lila consents to marry Russell and to settle down with him as his news photographer while he roams the world as a reporter.

REVIEWS: This is a fair program melodrama, centering around the machinations of an opportunistic young woman photographer whose rise to fame receives a jolt when, through no fault of her own, her reputation for being unfair causes her downfall. Like other pictures in which the voluptuous Cleo Moore has had the leading role, this one, too, has a lurid quality and is of a type that lends itself to sensational exploitation methods. As an entertainment, however, it is only moderately interesting and hardly believable. The story, which moves along at a leisurely pace, becomes highly melodramatic in the closing reels where Miss Moore, angered by the ill-luck that had befallen her, attempts to blackmail a powerful gangster with an incriminating photograph, only to be given a severe beating by his henchmen. The manner in which she is rescued by her boyfriend is as incongruous as the rest of the story. (*Harrison's Reports*)

CLEO WITH RAYMOND GREENLEAF AND EDDIE PARKER.

Here's a warning to nice pin-up girls seeking excitement on the other side of the camera. Blonde Cleo Moore decides to stop posing and start clicking. Her get-rich-quick tactics soon involve her in a broken romance and some underworld rough stuff. It's a footling plot. Buxom Cleo Moore makes the best of a sketchy part. Richard Crenna, a half-hearted boyfriend, convinces me that a camera is a girl's best friend. (*Picturegoer*)

When you have a star whose attributes are as celebrated as those of Cleo Moore and when the title of the picture in which she appears is *Over-Exposed*, what more do you want? Well, if you are an exhibitor or a member of the paying audience what you have a right to expect is a reasonable

amount of entertainment. Surprisingly enough, there is that too in this Lewis J. Rachmil production directed by Lewis Seiler. Since this is a low budget feature and not an art film, all ends happily with Miss Moore in Crenna's arms after his rescue of her from the hoods. Despite the rather silly plot, there are some very good performances by a more than competent cast of stock players. The story has the virtue of covering rather unfamiliar ground. And if the theatre owners can't exploit the aforementioned title and its coupling with Miss Moore they deserve to be demoted to television. The opening titles, incidentally, are extremely good. (*Hollywood Reporter*)

NOTES: In my opinion, *Over-Exposed* should have been filmed in color. It isn't the greatest screenplay, but it's very watchable. Cleo's acting is the best in her career. She looks stunning and her scenes with Raymond Greenleaf, as her mentor teaching her about the art of photography, are filled with chemistry between the two actors. Cleo is tough and likeable at the same time. However, there's less chemistry between Cleo and Richard Crenna. Partly for that reason the movie fails on impact. Nevertheless,

Over-Exposed is Cleo's best movie where she finally gets the chance to shine like a true movie star.

Richard Crenna (1926-2003), an award winning film, television and radio actor, was born in Los Angeles. He started out acting in TV shows before he made the step to acting in motion pictures. His career in films really took off in the mid-sixties. Crenna won several Golden Globe awards. Some of the films he appeared in are: *It Grows on Tress* (1952), *Made in Paris* (1966), *Wait Until Dark* (1967), *Body Heat* (1981) and *First Blood* (1982), *Rambo: First Blood Part II* (1985), *Rambo III* (1988), all with Sylvester Stallone.

Raymond Greenleaf (1892-1963) was acting on Broadway before he came to Hollywood in the 1940s. In the early 1920s he acted in summer stock theatre. His filmography includes: *Pinky* (1949), *East Side, West Side* (1949), *Storm Warning* (1951), *Ten Tall Men* (1951), *Angel Face* (1953) and *From the Terrace* (1960).

Over-Exposed was released on a double bill, in April 1956.

The National Legion of Decency rated the movie in category A-II and held no objection.

HIT AND RUN
1957 — United Artists
85 minutes — Black and White

DIRECTOR: Hugo Haas. PRODUCER: Hugo Haas. SCENARIO: Hugo Haas, based on an original story by Herbert Q. Phillips. PHOTOGRAPHY: Walter Strenge. MUSIC: Franz Steininger. EDITING: Stefan Arnsten. MAKEUP: Ted Coodley. SOUND: Earl Snyder. SCRIPT SUPERVISOR: Gloria Alexander. DIALOGUE SUPERVISOR: Mark Lowell.

CAST: **Cleo Moore** *(Julie Hilmer)*; Hugo Haas *(Gus Hilmer/twin brother)*; Vince Edwards *(Frank)*; Dolores Reed *(Miranda)*; Mari Lea *(Anita)*; Pat Goldin *(Undertaker)*; Carl Milletaire *(Lawyer)*; Robert Cassidy *(Sheriff)*; Dick Paxton *(Waiter)*; Julie Mitchum *(Circus Girl)*; John Zaremba *(Doctor)*; Steve Mitchell *(Bartender)*; Jan Englund *(Clara)*; Ella Mae Morse *(Singer)*; Kathy Marlowe, Vikki Dougan *(Girls)*.

STORY: Gus Hilmer, a middle-aged widower and owner of a garage, marries Julie, a sexy blonde showgirl down on her luck. The marriage causes a rift between Gus and Frank, his young mechanic and close friend, who believes that Julie is a gold-digger. Tension rises between Frank and Julie and he gives Gus notice that he is quitting. One night, while Gus is away from home, Frank makes a pass at Julie and reveals that he is passionately in love with her. She tries to keep him at bay out of loyalty to Gus, but his stronger will prevails and she gives in to his advances. Gus, a shady character himself, keeps secret the fact that he had an identical twin brother who had just been released from prison and meets the twin at a ramshackle house on the outskirts of town. Learning that Gus goes there, Frank secretly puts a scrapped car into working order and,

VINCE EDWARDS, CLEO AND HUGO HAAS.

practically compelling Julie to accompany him, rides out to the old house and deliberately runs down and kills Gus as he emerges from the building. He then takes the car back to a junk yard and disassembles it. Julie wants to tell the truth to the authorities, but Frank stops her. Shortly after Gus is buried, his twin brother shows up at the reading of the will and his likeness to Gus startles Julie. She and the twin share Gus's estate equally and he moves into a room in her room to help operate the gas station. Subtle remarks made by the twin regarding Julie's friendship with Frank leads her to suspect that he may be Gus and that the twin brother was the one killed by Frank. This is actually so, but Gus feeds her suspicions and eventually succeeds in trapping the lovers into admitting their guilt before revealing himself. With Julie and Frank taken into custody by the police, Frank turns his attention to a voluptuous lady lion-tamer who had been making a play for Frank.

REVIEWS: Paradoxically, a few more cooks might have helped the melodramatics brewed in *"Hit and Run."* With Hugo Haas handling a four-way chore, the plottage compounds a number of faults, resulting in a poor presentation overall. It's a minor entry for programmer sales. Too many of

CLEO AND VINCE EDWARDS.

the scenes written and directed by Haas have an ad lib quality and none of the performances is more than just adequate. (*Variety Daily*)

"*Hit and Run*" is not the greatest picture you are likely to see, but it reportedly was brought in at a fantastically low figure and, with the names Haas has assembled, it will probably do well for what it was designed — a double bill. Miss Moore is effective as the blonde time-bomb whose charms spark the murderous explosion and Vince Edwards is a strong leading man. Dolores Reed as the lion tamer, Mari Lea, Pat Goldin, Carl Millitaire and Robert Cassidy are notable in support. Rudi Feld's art direction achieves an especially mouldy kind of sordidness in backgrounds which Walter Strenge's camera catches very well. (*Hollywood Reporter*)

Accompanying [*The Delinquents*] at all houses is "*Hit and Run*," a United Artists release, which "had to explode." It did not. And the fault can't be Hugo Haas'. Director and heavy angle of the triangle, he is far too smooth a professional to drop the ball. Burly Vince Edwards isn't a bad actor either and even blonde Cleo Moore had come a long way since with a line. It's the picture. Another highly diluted "*Double Indemnity*." Too highly diluted. (*LA Times*)

Like the ingredients of most of the other films that have been written, produced and directed by Hugo Haas, in addition to his playing a leading role, this one, too, is made up of sex, lust and murder. It is a decidedly unpleasant and unwholesome entertainment, but it should go over fairly well with those adult movie-goers who enjoy lurid tales. The acting is good, but no sympathy is felt for any of the principal characters, not even the husband who is plotted against. The action takes place in a small town and the production values are modest. The photography is good. (*Harrison's Reports*)

A slight case of murder — or is it? A girl-chasing garage proprietor marries a showgirl (Cleo Moore). But there's a snag — his assistant is in love with her, too. Then the husband is killed and the lover thinks he's done it. But the plot keeps a trick up its sleeve. Hugo Haas directs, as well as acts the leading role and his skilful handling of the twist ending gives this brew a real kick. (*Picturegoer*)

NOTES: As early as October 1953, Haas had announced to make a movie called *Hit and Run*. The filming of *Hit and Run* had started as early as December 11, 1954. But because of Cleo's obligations at Columbia, the production was annulled. One year later, filming commenced. December 6, 1955 was the date mentioned that cameras would start rolling. On December 10, Vince Edwards was signed as the male lead. Later that month, Hugo signed pin-up model Dolores Reed (1932).

The movie opens with mechanic Gus having a good time at a nightclub. He's got his eye on showgirl Julie and sends his colleague Frank backstage to fetch her. Julie brushes him off. The nightclub's hostess talks her over. She mentions that Gus owns his own business and is loaded. With that said, Julie's expression changes. After a date in the nightclub, Julie visits Gus at work. He had promised to arrange her a car and Julie wants to

know if he can help her with finding one. She mentions that she needs a car to find another job. She quit working as a showgirl. Gus asks her to stay so he can help her find a job. They laugh amongst themselves when they discuss Gus's former marriage and make fun about his firm statement that he will never marry again. The next scene sees them stepping out of church where they just got married. With her moving in with Gus, the tension between Julie and Frank starts to build up. Although her motives seemed clear from the start, Julie's feelings towards Gus change, when she tries to fight off the attention Frank is giving her. Eventually she gives in, leading the situation to explode.

Hit and Run is a very tame movie. There's some chemistry between Vince Edwards and Cleo, sexy Dolores Reed has some nice scenes, showing off her physique. But Cleo's not the bad girl she was in her earlier efforts with Hugo Haas. Although I like the movie, I must say this is the most boring Haas-Moore outing.

Muscular Vince Edwards (1928-1996) started his career in B-movies. In the early 1950s he was under contract at Paramount for a while. He reached fame and recognition with his portrayal of a doctor in the TV series *Ben Casey* (1961-1966).

CLEO MOORE AND HUGO HAAS.

Kathy Marlowe (1934-2022) was a voluptuous blonde pin-up actress in the mold of Jayne Mansfield. Her biggest part was as *The Girl with an Itch* (1958). Kathy remembers working on *Hit and Run*. "That was one of my very first films. I became very good friends with Mr. Haas; he had this little doggie and his son Ivan. I remember him very well. Cleo Moore was the protégée of Hugo Haas. She was a little overweight, but she was nice."[32]

Cleo's sister Marilea made her second screen appearance in *Hit and Run*, having earlier appeared in *One Girl's Confession*. Said Cleo, "Just as I hoped, Marilea started college at UCLA this year, having won a dramatic scholarship from her fine work in high school plays. And just as she hoped, she also starts her movie career the same year with a big part in *Hit and Run*, which Hugo Haas is producing independently, and in which I co-star with Vince Edwards and Mr. Haas. She gives me a little trouble in the picture, too, because both of us are rivals for Vince's heart. I'm not going to tell you who gets him because it would give the plot away, but I can tell you that Marilea is giving me a run for the money in the acting department. I'm very proud of her."

The National Legion of Decency rated the movie in category A-II and held no objection.

32. Source: telephone conversation with author.

PUBLICITY STILL FOR
REMEMBER TO LIVE.

TELEVISION APPEARANCES

Los Angeles Dons Baseball Games
April 1948 — KTLA, sponsored by Standard Oil.

"Television will get a smattering of cheesecake when Standard Oil, sponsoring the Los Angeles Dons baseball games over KTLA, hits the airwaves. Standard has Cleo Moore, Miss Van Nuys introducing the commercials, on 16m film, in scant costume. Commercials will be viewed three times during the game."[33]

You Asked for It
1953 — ABC
"From Screen-test to Stardom" with Cleo Moore and Hugo Haas.

Hugo shows all the steps needed to make Cleo a star. He takes us behind the scenes of a screen test and Cleo acts in a scene with Burt Mustin. Also in the show, Dante, the Magician. He shows his ground-breaking sawing of a woman in half.

The "You Asked for It" TV show responded to requests from the viewer. Viewers were asked to send in postcards describing something they wanted to see on television. Hosted by Art Baker, it was initially titled "The Art Baker Show." The show was sponsored by *Skippy Peanut Butter* and *Studebaker Automobiles*.

33. *Variety*, April 21, 1948.

Strike it Rich
February 16, 1954 — CBS
Cleo *(herself)*, Warren Hull *(Host)*.

"Strike it Rich" is a game show where people in need of money appeared and told their misfortunes and then tried to win money by answering four questions.

The George Jessel Show
February 21, 1954 — ABC
Cleo *(herself)*, George Jessel *(himself)*.

"The George Jessel Show" ran for one season. It was broadcast live from New York.

Place the Face
September 25, 1954 — CBS
Cleo Moore *(contestant)*, Bill Cullen *(Host)*.

Quiz Show. Contestants were tasked with identifying people from their past who encountered them in a specific situation.

The Ford Television Theatre:
"Remember to Live"
November 4, 1954 — NBC
CAST: Dane Clark *(Joe Travis)*; Barbara Hale *(Marta Linden)*; Cleo Moore *(Lana)*; Judy Nugent *(Kathy Johnson)*; Richard Wessel *(Tom O'Brien)*; Paul Brinegar *(Hans)*; Ralph Peters *(Bert)*; Charles Watts *(Ed)*.

30-minute tele-novel. Following his return home, Korean War veteran Dane Clark cannot decide between the charms of curvaceous Lana and sedate Marta.

Sheilah Graham in Hollywood
March 4, 1955 — NBC

15-minute TV talk show hosted by columnist Sheilah Graham, who interviewed Cleo.

Strange Stories:
"Bed and Board"
October 29, 1956 — WPIX New York
CAST: Charles Coburn, Spring Byington, Cleo Moore, Mikel Conrad, Bill Edelson.

An older couple decide to turn their home into a boarding house. A husband makes good his promise to buy his wife a mansion. The catch is, he can only do so by taking in six boarders. This 30-minute program was originally a sitcom pilot made circa 1951, that apparently didn't air until it was broadcast as an episode in the anthology series "Strange Stories." The show was hosted by Edward Arnold.

Let's Play Golf
March 31, 1957 — KHJ-TV

"Joe Kirkwood Jr. may have a little trouble keeping his mind on the game when he takes over the job of teaching the pulchritudinous Cleo Moore the lore of the links on today's show."

PIN-UPS AND PORTRAITS

254 "ONE GIRL'S CONFESSION"

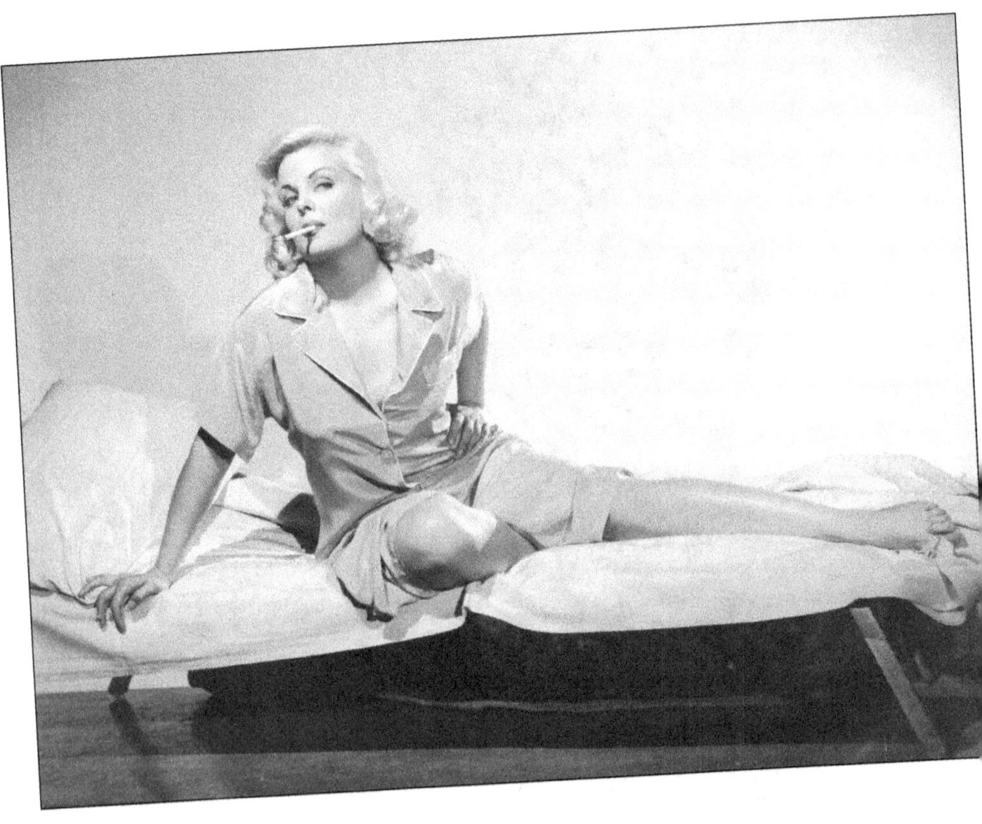

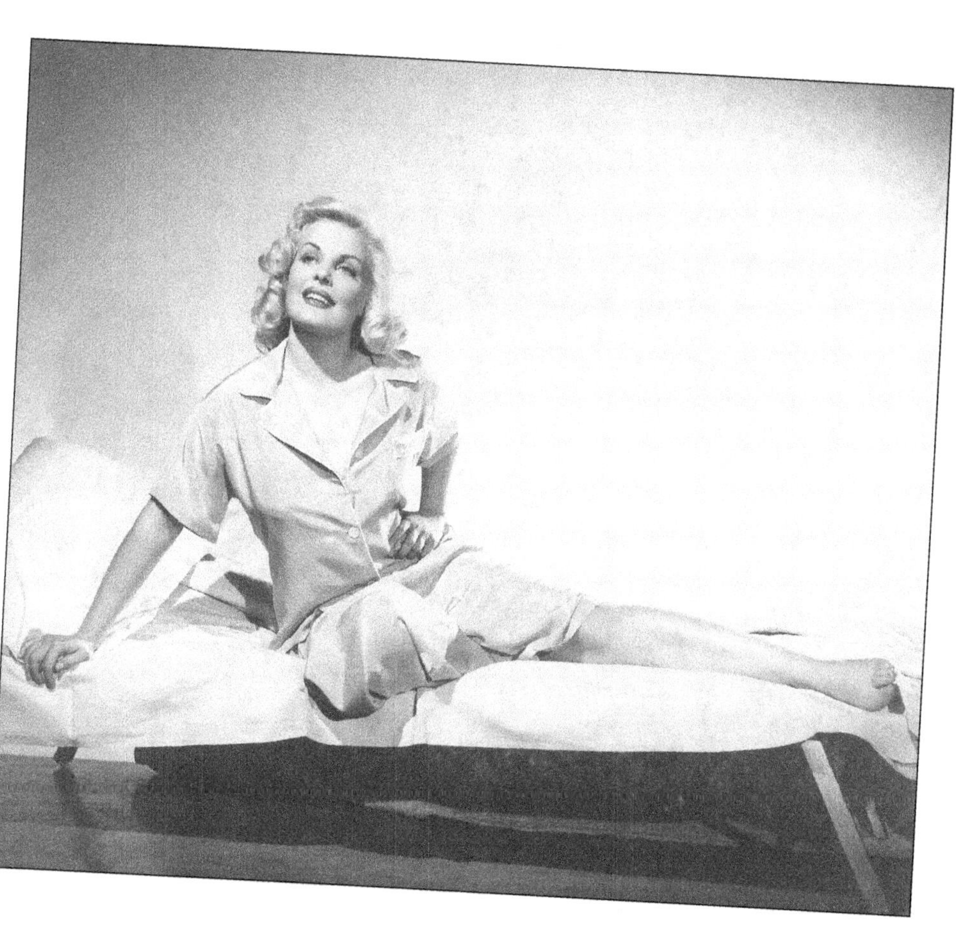

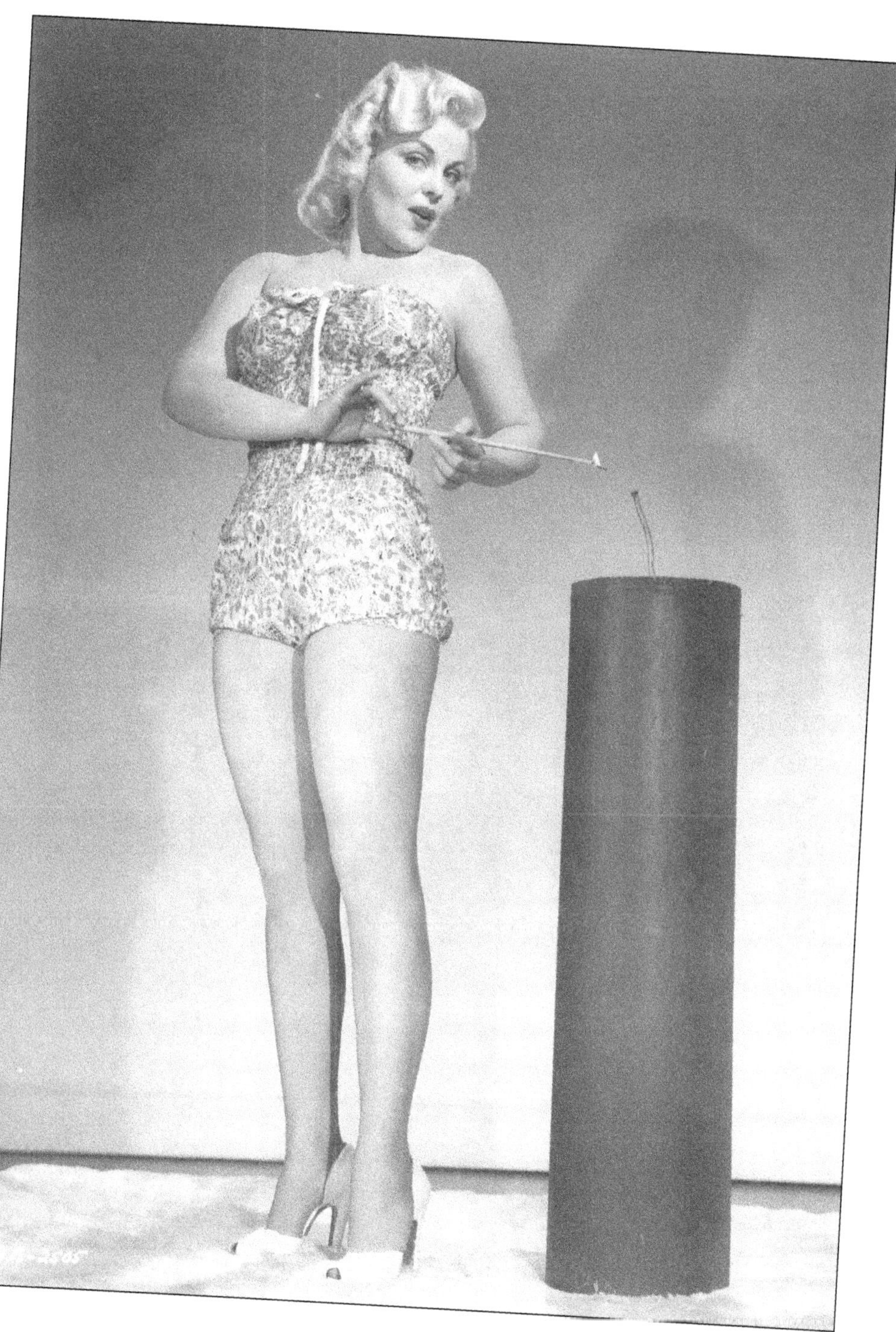

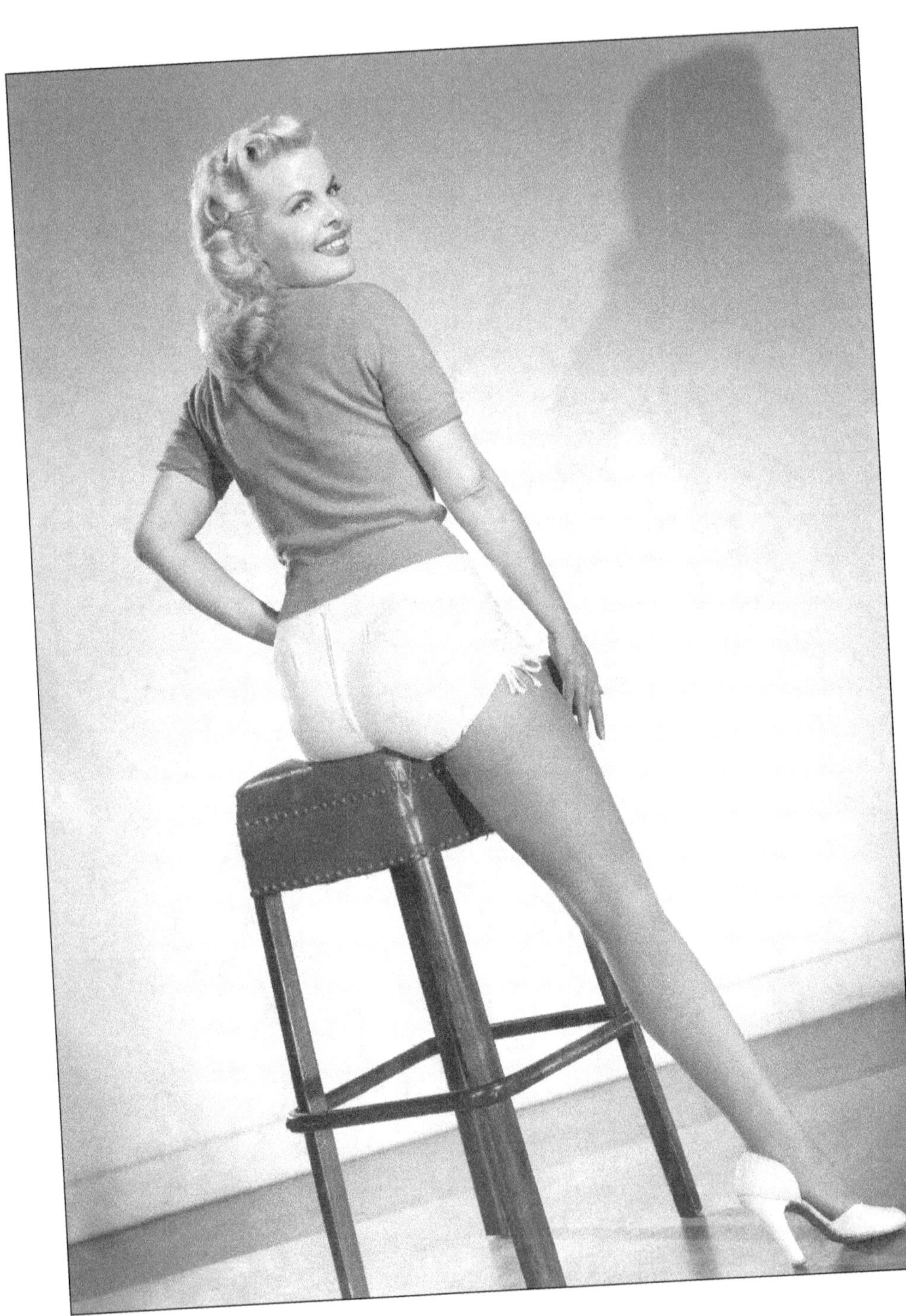

282 **"ONE GIRL'S CONFESSION"**

284 "ONE GIRL'S CONFESSION"

MAGAZINE COVERS

DON'T LEGALIZE PROSTITUT
(SEE PAGE
Focus
OCT.
25c
Town and Country
EVERY ADULT SHOULD READ:
LIQUOR CAN RUIN YOUR SEX LIFE!
SUNBATHING CAN SHORTE
Murder at a NUDIST

FACING PAGE:
OCTOBER 1950, USA.

TOP TO BOTTOM:
APRIL 20, 1952, ITALY.
MAY 1952, USA.
MAY 1953, ITALY.

TOP TO BOTTOM:
JUNE 1954, USA.
JULY 5, 1954, USA.
NOVEMBER 27, 1954, UK.

FACING PAGE:
MAY 10, 1955, UK.

THE MYSTERIOUS SEX PHOBIAS
MAN to MAN
THE WEIRD BEAST THAT TERRIFIED FRANCE
OTS DELUXE

SEX ATTRACTION SECRETS
TEMPO
NEWS WEEKLY · JULY 5, 1954
15¢
INSIDE STORY OF THE PUCKER-UP GIRL

EVERY THURSDAY 3ᵈ
Picturegoer
THE NATIONAL FILM WEEKLY
I'LL OPEN YOUR EYES ON HOLLYWOOD
BY
RITA GAM
Working with
Shelley Winters
by
JOHN GREGSON

SHE MAY REIGN WHERE BULLETS RULED

By Pat Jameson

BULLETS don't bother bosomy Cleo Moore. This platinum blonde film star plans to plant her tootsies in the bloodstained footprints of the "Kingfish" —Huey Long, America's rough, tough, dictator, who ruled her home State of Louisiana with a machine gun till he was shot dead 20 years ago.

Cleo, who was once married to Huey's son Palmer —aims to be Governor of Louisiana.

Friends forecast fireworks if her wish comes true— but she'll have to be a hydrogen bomb- shell if she's going to match the rum- pus her notorious father - in - law kicked up when he held that office.

HUEYS career was short and violent. He be- came known throughout the world as a criminal, a clown, a play-boy and above all, a power-mad politician.

JUSTICE NEVER OVERTOOK HIM, THE "KINGFISH"—AS HUEY CALLED HIMSELF— WAS AS SLIPPERY AS AN EEL.

"Not even his mother could pin anything on that bouncing boy," said the cynics.

Huey could wriggle his way out of any situation —except the fatal one that occurred when a fanatical young doctor fired a revolver at him point-blank. A few seconds later the assassin died, riddled with 63 machine-gun bullets. The "Kingfish's" henchman had done his last job too late.

Huey Long's death two days later at the age of forty-two marked the end of seven years of fear and cor- ruption in Louisiana.

Brutal secret police used Ges- tapo methods to make sure that nobody overthrew the dictator. You could not teach in a school or open a restaurant if you weren't on the "right side" of the paunchy red-haired Governor. You never asked questions if your rela- tives or friends were evicted from their homes, lost their jobs, or even disappeared. You knew with- out asking that they had opposed the "Kingfish" in some way.

ONCE, when his candidate was defeated in an election in the jazz-mad city of New Orleans. Huey rode in with an army of gun- happy guards. With machine guns ready to mow down any opposition, the "Kingfish" put his man in control.

It's little wonder that he was a marked man. He knew it. Four square-jawed young men slept at his bed- room door and travel- led in his car, revol- vers always at the ready.

There were times

Cleo Moore is soar- ing to success. She has played several film leads. Now she plans to take a lead in the politics of her home State, Louisiana.

when Huey's pudgy face felt what it was like to be at the re- ceiving end of a solid punch. He would often arrive at his office with a black eye or a bloody nose after a brawl at one of Wash- ington's supposedly fashionable night clubs.

But most people restrained them- selves, and almost stowed their dis- like by leaving the building when he arrived.

Huey could never stop talking.

This came in useful in his chosen career of politics. Once he spoke for 15¹⁄₂ hours in the American Senate, consuming 15 glasses of milk, one and a half pounds of grapes and half a pound of cheese to keep him- self going.

THE "KINGFISH" PROM- ISES WERE FABULOUS. "EVERY MAN A KING" WAS HIS MOTTO, AND WITH THIS IN MIND HE SAID HE WOULD GIVE EVERY MAN A JOB, A HOUSE, A CAR, AN INCOME OF £400 A YEAR— AND "TWO CHICKENS IN THE POT."

He never lived to keep these promises—but he did trans- form the backward State of Louisiana in his few years of power. New schools, hospitals, clinics and a state university sprang up as if by magic. The state debt sprang up too—from £2 million to £50 million. A million-pound Capitol building was constructed as the centre of administra- tion in Baton Rouge. Decorated with 26 different kinds of marble, it was finished in less than 12 months.

BORN in a log cabin in the backwoods. Huey Long was popu- lar with country folk. He must have forgotten the basic facts of farm life when he promised them— "I'll transact every com- male and female—for ticks."

But though he slipped up on the sex-life of cattle, the "Kingfish" improved transport in the country districts He replaced the dirt roads with concrete highways —pointedly avoiding areas hostile to his rule.

ONCE Huey Long's antics almost caused an inter- national "situation." Gorgeous with gold braid and stiff with dignity, the commander of a French ship on an official visit to New Orleans, called on the Governor.

The "Kingfish" received him— in green silk pyjamas. Furious, the Frenchman called him a "barbarian" and stormed back to his ship.

Cleo scores over her father-in-law there. She'd be one Governor whose pyjamas would raise no objections from any sailor.

Australasian
POST
APRIL 5, 1956
Registered at the G.P.O., Melbourne, for
transmission by post as a newspaper.
1'-
WEEKLY

FACING PAGE:
APRIL 5, 1956, AUSTRALIA.

TOP TO BOTTOM:
JANUARY 1956, USA.
APRIL 1956, USA.
DECEMBER 7, 1955, FRANCE.

GONDEL
Yirminci
ASıR
DAS MODERNE JOURNAL
Folge 67
XII/57
DM 1,50
S. 10,—

TOP TO BOTTOM:
JUNE 1956, GERMANY.
DECEMBER 13, 1956, TURKEY.
DECEMBER 1957, GERMANY.

FACING PAGE:
JANUARY 1957, USA.

e Truth About Sex Energy
IT!
nual
Madria
gapore
Winter
1957
35c
ial report on
ESBIANS

TOP TO BOTTOM:
MARCH 1957, USA.
UNKNOWN MONTH 1959, FRANCE.
DECEMBER 1961, USA.

FACING PAGE:
UNKNOWN MONTH 1965, FRANCE.

BOLD
15¢
ANC
MARCH 1957

nor
chants
LD'S
EDEST
N
eo Moore

FOLIES DE 28 PAGES N° 152
Paris Hollywood
250

69
PHOTOS
EXCLUSIVES

DEC. PDC 35¢
Foto-rama
All New! More Fotos!
More Features!
Exclusive:
CASTRO PROVES
HITLER IN BRAZIL!
WHY GIRLS GO
ALL THE WAY
WITH SINATRA!

DE   32 PAGES ★ N° 206
Hollywood
INTERDITE A L'AFFICHAGE
AUX MINEURS DE 18 ANS
FOIS PAR MOIS   PRIX : 3 NF
FRANÇAISE ET ÉTRANGER.. 3,50 NF

BIBLIOGRAPHY

Barbour, Alan G. *Cliffhanger — A Pictorial History of the Motion Picture Serial*. New York: A&W Publishers, Inc., 1977.

Barbour, Alan G. *Congo Bill*. Hollywood: Serial Quarterly, April-June 1967.

Cocchi, John. *Second Features — The Best of the 'B' Films*. New York: Citadel Press, 1991.

Doggett, Dannielle. *Cut! Hollywood murders, accidents, and other tragedies*. New York: Barron's, 2006.

Kleno, Larry. *Kim Novak on Camera*. New York: A.S. Barnes & Company, Inc., 1980.

Koper, Richard. *Fifties Blondes — Sexbombs, Sirens, Bad Girls and Teen Queens*. BearManor Media: Duncan, Oklahoma, 2010.

Loutzenhiser, James K. *Hugo Haas — Sincere Artist Who Became Lost in the Hollywood Shuffle*. New York: Films in Review, February 1978.

Silver, Alan and Ward, Elizabeth. *Film Noir — An Encyclopedic Reference Guide*. London: Bloomsbury, 1988.

Weldon, Michael. *The Psychotronic Encyclopedia of Film*. New York: Ballantine Books, 1983.

INDEX

Monroe, Marilyn 16, 48, 50, 54, 57, 62, 63,
    64, 75, 76, 84, 85, 93, 99, 125, 144, 168.
Moore, Jonnie Mae 11, 18, 19, 31, 47, 103,
    112, 114.
Moore, Mary Lea 30, 105, 111, 114, 146,
    147, 238, 245.
Moore, Murphy 27, 28, 31, 32, 35, 37, 41, 42,
    44, 112, *113*.
Moore, Terry 68, 161, 164.
Moore, Una 25, 27, 28, 30-32, 37, 41, 42,
    103, 110, *113*.
Moore, Yvonne Inez 29, 30, 42, 46, 47, 103,
    106, 112, 114.
Nichols, Barbara 84, 144.
Novak, Kim 23, 76, 84, 85, 88, 91, 97.
O'Brien, Edmond *143*, 144.
Pall, Gloria 57.
Parsons, Louella 57, 60.

Riordan, Christopher 125.
Rodriguez, Juan 103, 106, 108.
Sharpe, Karen 60, 181, 186, 188.
Simonelli, Charles 80,
Sterling, Jan 76, 144, 222, *224*, *226-229*, 230.
Tone, Franchot *84*.
Travis, Tony *See*: Kleefeld, Tony.
Vallin, Rick *124*, 154, 156, 181, *186*, 187,
    188.
Van Doren, Mamie 16, 23, 79, 131, 179, 213.
West, Mae 72, 117.
Wilson, Marie 19, 42.
Winchell, Walter 103, 104.
Zanuck, Darryl F. 68, 75.